PENGUIN BUSINESS
THE WISEST OWL

Anupam Gupta is a chartered accountant, author and podcast host. He worked for two decades as an investment research analyst and as a thematic research consultant in institutional equities with leading brokerages such as CLSA, HDFC Securities, Barclays and Ambit Capital. In 2020, Anupam, with Saurabh Mukherjea, co-authored the bestselling book *The Victory Project: Six Steps to Peak Potential.* Since 2017, Anupam has been hosting *Paisa Vaisa*, a free-to-air personal finance podcast available on all podcasting platforms. *Paisa Vaisa* has almost 2 million downloads and won the Best Business Podcast award at the Asia Podcast Awards held in 2019.

T0021032

THE WISEST OWL

OWL

BE YOUR OWN
FINANCIAL
PLANNER

Foreword by
SAURABH MUKHERJEA

ANUPAM GUPTA

BUSINESS

An imprint of Penguin Random House

PENGUIN BUSINESS

USA | Canada | UK | Ireland | Australia
New Zealand | India | South Africa | China

Penguin Business is part of the Penguin Random House group of companies
whose addresses can be found at global.penguinrandomhouse.com

Published by Penguin Random House India Pvt. Ltd
4th Floor, Capital Tower 1, MG Road,
Gurugram 122 002, Haryana, India

Penguin
Random House
India

First published in Penguin Business by Penguin Random House India 2022

ISBN 9780143455905

Typeset in Adobe Caslon Pro by Manipal Technologies Limited, Manipal
Printed at Replika Press Pvt. Ltd, India

www.penguin.co.in

For my family: my mother, Shubhra Saran, my wife, Vanita, and my son, Varun

'The main thing about money, Bud, it makes you do things you don't want to do.'

—Lou Mannheim (Hal Holbrook) to Bud Fox (Charlie Sheen), *Wall Street* (1987)

'It ain't what you don't know that gets you into trouble. It's what you know for sure that just ain't so.'

—Opening lines from the movie *The Big Short* (2015)

Contents

Foreword   xiii

Preface   xxv

1. A Brave New World   1
    Adviser Perspectives: Dilshad Billimoria   13
2. *Kal, Aaj Aur Kal*   21
    Adviser Perspectives: Harsh Roongta   34
3. How Fintechs Changed Personal Finance   43
    Adviser Perspectives: Lovaii Navlakhi   55
4. The FIRE Dream   63
    Adviser Perspectives: Melvin Joseph   75
5. A Framework for the Future   82
    Adviser Perspectives: Suresh Sadagopan   91
6. Checklists for My Money   99
    Adviser Perspectives: Vishal and Shalini Dhawan   118

Acknowledgements   127
Notes   131
References   137

Foreword

Change is a continuous process. You can discern a change only once in a generation. Because once you discern it, you are already there. So in these last 50 years I can discern only two changes, but they are large because a continuous process is being focussed at two or three points. The next big change will come with my son. There are spans of transition. There are much bigger spans with the succeeding generations.

My son will go through a very large change in circumstances in many ways. In the family, in the school surroundings, in the job market, everywhere. I grew up in a half ritualistic background. My son will have no ritualistic background. But if my son loses the rituals even further, he could still be rooted locally, within his peer group. There will be many like him. Society is moving that way.

—V.S. Naipaul, *A Million Mutinies Now*, 1990

Very few books capture the vastness of India, let alone the diversity and the far-reaching impact of generational changes. The paragraphs quoted above are from a book written as far

back as 1990. Many of us in our late forties or early fifties
romanticize the change that our generation has seen post-
Liberalization in 1991—that life has changed for the better.
But India had seen gut-wrenching change even before that,
as you can read in the two paragraphs quoted above, taken
from Naipaul's conversation with Pravas, an engineer who
was thinking of university education and a career in 1962.
Visceral, transformative change in India happens every once in
a generation. We are in the midst of one such change now—
the shift of savings towards financial assets from physical assets
such as gold and real estate. This is an important change that
will play out for many years to come since India has a long way
to go from unremunerative and unproductive investments like
real estate and gold towards equities.

We set up Marcellus Investment Managers in late 2018,
and our travel of the past four years—where we met tens of
thousands of affluent Indian families and high-net-worth
individuals (HNIs)—has convinced us of this powerful
generational change. We have written about this change in
several publications, including *Coffee Can Investing: The Low
Risk Road to Stupendous Wealth* (by myself, Rakshit Ranjan and
Pranab Uniyal) in 2018, and *Diamonds in the Dust: Consistent
Compounding for Extraordinary Wealth Creation* (by myself,
Rakshit Ranjan, and Salil Desai) in 2021. Our travel and
research over most of these past few years have convinced us
that the shift toward financial assets is not only inevitable but
essential for Indian families to prepare themselves better for their
retirement. Even the RBI, in their 2017 Household Survey, has
warned of the deleterious effect of going into retirement laden
with real estate and gold. The RBI personnel are not known to
be alarmist in their use of the English language. So when they
write a paragraph such as the one below, it suggests that they
are really concerned about this issue:

Over the coming decade and a half, the elderly cohort is expected to grow by 75 percent. Only a small fraction of this cohort has saved in private pension plans. Moreover, a large segment of the population of households in all age cohorts has not actively taken steps to insure adequate financial coverage during retirement. The need to finance adequate consumption during retirement is therefore a looming issue, and when combined with the low penetration of insurance, households appear particularly vulnerable to adverse shocks later in life.

What drives the pre-eminence of physical assets—real estate and gold—when it comes to Indian households' investments? In our book *Diamonds in the Dust*, my colleagues and I and bust four myths that we encountered during our meetings with HNIs, myths which we believe have driven Indian households to invest in real estate and gold:

Myth 1: Gold will help me protect my wealth.

Reality: This is patently wrong since the BSE Sensex has outperformed gold in most long-term time periods. The 2017 RBI report also makes a case for reallocation of wealth from gold to other financial assets.

Myth 2: Real estate will help me grow my wealth.

Reality: Home prices have at best kept pace with consumer inflation. Moreover, with residential rental yields (2–3 per cent) being far above home loan rates (7 per cent), there is room for home prices to correct going forward. Besides, investment in real estate is cumbersome, illiquid and saddled with high transaction costs.

Myth 3: Debt mutual funds offer decent returns with low volatility.

Reality: This myth has been perpetrated by armies of salespeople who show debt fund returns as 'safer' than equities with returns 'higher' than fixed deposits. However, the shuttering of some prominent mutual fund schemes (following investments in high-risk, low-quality paper in their debt funds) has busted this myth.

Myth 4: GDP growth drives the stock market. So, if I (or my wealth manager) can time the economic cycle, I can time the stock market.

Reality: As we have shown in our research (Marcellus, 2019), the relationship between GDP growth and earnings growth of the NSE Nifty 50 has broken down in the recent past. The Nifty does not capture the dynamism in India's economy, considering that in the past decade (2011-2020) the Nifty has lagged nominal GDP growth in terms of price performance.

While the negation of these myths results in a strong case in favour of equity investments, equities also suffer from drawbacks such as lack of good advice and dodgy products being peddled as safe. As we have explained in *Diamonds in the Dust*, investors in the Indian stock market need to minimize risk (such as accounting risks, revenue risks, profit risks and liquidity risks) while investing in equities. The approach that we, at Marcellus, follow is the consistent compounding formula of investing in clean, well-managed Indian companies selling essential products behind very high barriers of entry. My belief in this investment approach has resulted in my investing my savings, my parents' savings and that of several thousand Indian families—whose savings Marcellus manages—as per this approach.

What approach you should follow depends on your priorities and goals. The last thing you want to do is get carried away with the noise of screaming TV channels and the flood of content on social media. Long-term financial planning is built to take you through life, not just the latest bull market. As we explained in *Coffee Can Investing*, it is important to link your investment style with your financial objectives; otherwise you will end up either taking unnecessary risks or undershooting your financial goals. The essential link between your investment style and your financial objective is made through financial planning.

There are two ways to start your financial plan, depending on your objectives and the stage of life that you are at. For beginners, it makes sense to use the DIY approach because that helps you learn important concepts in personal finance, such as risk, return, liquidity, etc., and also sets you on the path of rigorous discipline towards retirement planning. But as you grow older and your responsibilities increase, you might need help from a professional. Indeed, most of the incorrect decisions that we make with regard to our investments, usually stem from misinformed (even if well-intentioned) advice from friends, family and social groups. Cocktail parties during bull markets tend to drive more decisions than conversations with investment professionals. And this is so prevalent that legendary fund manager Peter Lynch had a cocktail-party theory that he wrote about in his seminal book *One Up on Wall Street* (Lynch & Rothchild, 1989). Lynch used cocktail-party conversations as indicators of forward stock market returns, starting from Stage One, when no one at cocktail parties was interested in him or his profession (and hence the market was likely to turn up), all the way to Stage Four, when the same people would tell him what stocks he should buy (and hence an indicator that the market was due for a tumble).

Lynch wrote his book in 1989, when there was no social media, and his theory, I reckon, holds true even today. As more investors enter the stock market, the urge to know how the stock market will perform is even higher. It is a futile chase. As I have written time and again, timing the market is neither feasible nor is it the primary driver of long-term investment returns. As explained in Chapter 6 of *Diamonds in the Dust* (titled 'When to Buy'), once you buy clean companies that can grow earnings consistently via their competitive advantages and smart capital allocation, timing the stock price or the broader market is taken out of the equation. Using extensive research and analysis, we showed that timing the overall market is not worth the effort and surely not worth testing your luck in getting each buy and sell timing right. What matters is the quality of the stocks that you are investing in and the regularity with which you keep investing your savings in the stock market.

And thankfully, with rising awareness among young Indians regarding the merits of equity investing, the idea of low-cost regular investment is gathering pace. There are three major changes here that are very positive and encouraging in building a culture of investing in India.

- First, the Systematic Investment Plan (SIP) has exploded in popularity, with the number of accounts reaching a record high (Dhawan, 2022) of 5.39 crore in April 2022. SIPs are an easy way to invest regularly in the markets, and the mutual fund industry's efforts to popularize this simple product appear to have paid off.
- Second, the rise of the passive investment industry in India—passive products totalled more than Rs 5 lakh crore (Roy, 2022) at the end of April 2022. The passive

investment industry has been gaining popularity globally as delivering index-beating returns becomes more and more difficult and investors question the high costs arising from active asset management. Jack Bogle, Vanguard's legendary founder, knew the importance of costs in mutual funds, and his idea of the humble index fund is now firmly rooted in India.

- And third, the rise of the National Pension Scheme (NPS). I firmly believe that if the Indian stock market is to be taken to the masses, the highly successful National Pension Scheme construct looks to be the most likely vehicle which can serve this purpose. Widespread adoption of the NPS will give India something akin to the 401(k) in the United States which has driven the massification of equity investment there.

I believe that the trends outlined above are structurally positive changes in habits that will help build a culture of staying committed in the long term to stock markets. And to be sure, this culture will be tested in the long run as stock markets are also prone to upheavals that can test the patience of veterans and amateurs alike. This is where knowledge, learning and good advice come in.

Anupam and I have known each other for a decade now—a decade in which we have co-authored with each other dozens of notes and one bestselling book, *The Victory Project: Six Steps to Peak Potential* (2020). I have also seen at first hand how Anupam has built a franchise around his award-winning personal finance podcast *Paisa Vaisa*, which has a fan base well beyond the geographical borders of India, thanks to Anupam's ability to take abstract concepts and simplify them.

In this book, Anupam has delved into how to start learning more about personal finance in general and equity investments in particular. The obsession with equity investments tends to blind us to basic financial products like insurance, credit cards, etc. There are major life decisions—such as buying (or renting) a home, education for our children, building a retirement corpus, etc.—which require us to be well versed in how financial products work. Hence, it is important to build a strong base of learning around all financial products that affect your life, not just stock markets. Building this basic knowledge of personal finance products is relatively straightforward, and Anupam has spent a significant part of this book explaining how this base can be done.

But self-learning will only take you so far. India is a young country, and preceding generations have relied on their own wisdom or that of friends and family—and we've seen the results of that. While the distribution community and financial intermediaries in India have done yeoman service in introducing and spreading mass-market products like insurance and mutual funds across the length and breadth of the country, this work has only begun. Penetration levels are still low, and the financialization of savings will take many years to play out.

What hobbles the process of financializing savings is advice. Good personal finance advice remains hard to find in India, and investors find it difficult to trust advisers and intermediaries, given that mis-selling by intermediaries is—despite the best intentions of regulators—still a problem. Deepti Bhaskaran and Monika Halan, in an article for *Mint* in 2013, estimated that more than Rs 1.56 trillion leaked out of the insurance industry because of investors letting their policies lapse over a seven-year period ending 2011–12. 'The actual loss is likely to be a multiple of that,' the authors wrote. While the insurance industry and investor awareness have come a long way since then, the value of good advice should be appreciated by readers. Thus, self-learning is a good start, but good advice will help you avoid landmines and point you in the right direction.

But where does one get good advice? While generic advice is as old as our parents telling us to buy a home with our first salary, the area of fee-only financial advice is relatively new. SEBI's investment adviser (IA) regulations were first released in 2013 and amended in 2020. The registered investment advisor (RIA) is paid by the client and hence works in the client's interest. This is fundamentally different from an intermediary who is paid for by the product manufacturer whose product he or she sells and hence his services (and recommendations) are free to you. While this model worked well in selling insurance and mutual funds across India, there was a misalignment of incentives, because what was sold by the intermediary wasn't necessarily the best product for you, resulting in the bad advice and losses to investors mentioned earlier.

Obviously, not all intermediaries work against the client's interest, otherwise poor performance of their recommendations would hurt their reputation as well. Indeed, the mutual fund industry has worked well with the massive mutual fund distributor (MFD) community in filling gaps and addressing issues. But as people understand financial products better, they will value unbiased advice, and SEBI is moving in the right direction with the RIA regulations.

RIA is still a young profession, given that the regulations came out less than a decade ago. However, India already has a clutch of genuine, client-focused, fee-only RIAs who are working to provide holistic services and lifetime financial planning. Anupam has interviewed six of these advisers who are reputed names in the industry. I found these adviser perspectives to be the real juice in the book. The advisers give their insights on important decisions that are familiar to all of us: rent or buy our own home, stocks or mutual funds, active or passive investing, etc. Readers will find these perspectives useful, especially given the polarized discussions that abound on these topics. The final section of the book consists of useful advice in the form of questionnaires and calculations that could help readers in making their own financial plans.

India's economic transformation continues to be remarkable. In fact, as I write this foreword, *The Economist* has hailed India as the world's fastest-growing large economy and said that India is likely to hold this position for several years to come. Millions have been lifted out of poverty in the past few decades, and while COVID-19 ravaged the economically weaker sections of society, the economic recovery that followed has been remarkable. There will be headwinds for sure, but history has shown us that dedicated, honest and committed entrepreneurs use these challenges to embark on and expand their ventures.

As we wrote in Marcellus Investment Managers' research notes, the Russia–Ukraine war has rekindled the prospect of another Cold War, which could split the world into an authoritarian bloc (China, Russia, Pakistan, etc.) versus a democratic bloc (the USA, EU, UK, India, etc.). This could, in turn, result in the Asian version of NATO and a consequent quid pro quo between the various countries in the democratic bloc. India is well positioned to benefit economically from this arrangement in the form of increased foreign direct investments (FDI), foreign portfolio investments (FPI) and trade inflows (largely in the form of the Western world outsourcing much of its white-collar office work in IT services, finance, HR, payroll and marketing to India) in return for continued allegiance to the democratic bloc. Formal sector job creation could, therefore, benefit greatly from this increase in outsourcing.

As more jobs are created, there will be a greater demand to know more about money. While previous generations were happy giving their first paychecks to their family, subsequent generations would want to be on a road of financial independence right from the first day of their jobs. Hence, there will always be demand for good financial advice and sound knowledge around basic precepts—such as risk, return, inflation, liquidity, etc.—for all of us. This book arms readers with a road map on how to get started and how basic financial plans work. At the other end, as high-net-worth individuals realize the futility in low-yielding, illiquid investments such as real estate, they will look for advisers with high integrity and trust to form long-lasting client–adviser relationships. This book has six in-depth interviews with advisers on how they work in building these relationships.

In our 2020 book *The Victory Project,* Anupam and I have outlined 'The Simplicity Paradigm', which has core concepts such as specialize, simplify, spiritualize, on which we built behaviours such as declutter, creativity, collaboration. The book propagates a lifestyle of focus and hard work that helps us make a successful profession out of doing things that we inherently love and are good at. In a large free-market economy like India, the rewards for being successful at doing what we love are significant, as we have shown in the book. Hence, focusing on your profession or vocation and sticking to a well-developed financial plan that helps you achieve your goals is a much more fulfilling approach to life than constantly obsessing over the direction of India's economy, the future of the stock market and whether your portfolio is beating that of your friend. This book gives you very high-quality material to help you embark on your personal finance journey and stay the course.

May 2022   Saurabh Mukherjea,
Mumbai   Founder and chief investment officer,
                                       Marcellus Investment Managers

Preface

One crore new Demat accounts were opened (Sultana & Ramarathinam, *Mint*, 2021) in FY21—more than the previous two years combined. By the time this book goes to print, tens of lakhs more would have been opened. All you need today to buy stocks or mutual funds is a smartphone and an Internet connection, along with basic compliance documents. India is slowly but surely making a shift towards financial assets (stocks and mutual funds) and away from old-school physical assets (real estate and gold). If you're not part of this shift yet, you will be, eventually.

India is traversing a generation gap of epic proportions. In 1977, Reliance Industries' IPO created an equity cult. In 2021, Zerodha added more customers in October[1] than it did in its first seven years, and a whole bunch of new-age start-ups, such as Policybazaar, Nykaa, Zomato, and Paytm listed on the bourses. The gap between the publishing of the book (Basu & Dalal, 1993) *The Scam: Who Won, Who Lost, Who Got Away* and the release of the brilliant web series[2] *Scam 1992: The Harshad Mehta Story*, based on the book, is twenty-seven years. India has changed profoundly during this time. Our population is much younger—half of today's India was born after 1995. The new generations of Indians entering the workforce demand more knowledge on their investments—and social media is full of solutions. But it is difficult to separate signal from noise, to learn useful things, and to derive actionable advice from a world overflowing with content. The first step in working towards your financial goals is to build a strong foundation.

This book will help you set that foundation. This book is the result of extensive interactions with some of India's veteran financial advisers. Here's how I chose them.

Methodology Followed in This Book

I was extremely lucky to be helped on this part by the meticulous and diligent Deepti Bhaskaran, veteran personal finance journalist who has now branched out in the health-tech space. Deepti worked for more than eleven years at the *Mint* newspaper, where she was also editor, personal finance. Deepti is highly regarded in the personal finance community, and I thank her for her significant contribution in helping me develop the methodology that follows.

Step 1: I focused only on SEBI-registered investment advisers (RIAs). This means that mutual fund distributors (MFDs) are not part of this exercise, even though they can offer limited financial advice. I excluded MFDs because they are paid by the mutual fund companies and not by their clients. This is not a testimony to their abilities because, in my conversations with industry experts and retail investors, I found that there are many MFDs who are doing an outstanding job on advice. However, MFD advice is limited to investments, and for the purposes of this book, I wanted holistic financial planners (refer to Step 3). Similarly, certified financial planners (CFPs) registered under the Financial Planning Standards Board (FPSB) are also not part of this exercise, as a) FPSB's parent body is based in the USA and not India, b) CFPs can apply for RIA licences, and hence, those CFPs who are RIAs are already included in my exercise. Thus, I looked at SEBI's RIA database[3] on 31 July 2021, at which time there were around 1330 RIAs.

Step 2: I focused only on those SEBI RIAs whose addresses (as per the SEBI RIA database linked to above) are in the four metro cities (Delhi, Chennai, Kolkata, Mumbai) and Bengaluru. I admit that in the digital era, the location of your adviser is probably irrelevant but as this is a voluntary effort, my resources are limited and hence I focused only on these large cities. Even so, this left me with a list of around 780, which is a majority of the original 1330 RIAs.

Step 3: Of these 780, I excluded those RIAs who offer only investment advice, or services such as portfolio management, equity advisory, stock tips, trading ideas, etc. Instead, I looked for those who offered the entire gamut of financial planning services, including investment advisory. These services start with basic risk profiling and cover almost every financial product that you own. The idea is to align your (and your family's) life and goals to your finances, keeping in mind your risk profile. This process is far more exhaustive and longer term than investment advisory. To get an idea of the range of services, you can check out the websites of the advisers mentioned in this book.

Step 4: Of those remaining, I applied a filter of a minimum of seven years of work experience as a SEBI RIA. SEBI's RIA rules were introduced in 2013 and hence, the RIAs considered for my exercise should have an RIA licence dating back latest till 2015 (seven years prior to 2022). To further strengthen their credentials, I gave extra weightage to those RIAs who had deeper experience in financial planning. Thus, as you will notice, almost all the RIAs interviewed in this book launched their financial planning firm in the early 2000s, except for Harsh Roongta (who was running Apnaloan.com at that time) and Melvin Joseph (who was working at senior positions in the banking, financial services and insurance, or BFSI, industry at that time). Persistency of customers (i.e., how long a customer stayed with an RIA) also played a key role as a qualifying criterion.

Step 5: Finally, Deepti and I reached out to the BFSI industry to vet the shortlisted candidates. We spoke with many veterans and experts to get an idea of the state of the adviser industry and what it takes to be a good adviser. We realized that using the term 'best financial adviser' for our book is a highly subjective process and we admit that these are the 'best' in our opinion based on limited quantitative data (number of years of experience) and extensive qualitative data (depth of experience, range of services, industry reputation, persistency of customers, etc.).

Hence, choosing India's best financial advisers is not the same as choosing, say, India's best stocks or India's best mutual funds. That process would be easier because the best stocks or the best mutual funds are those that create the highest amount of wealth over a specific period. Instead, our process was more subjective and more qualitative. We do not judge the quality of an RIA on the returns that his financial plan creates but on the quality of service that he or she offers to his client over the length of their relationship and the reputation that the adviser has earned over their long years of service. Choosing the final list of six RIAs was a tough and arduous process as we excluded some outstanding RIAs from our list, because they had less than seven years of RIA experience. We vigorously encourage you to choose your RIA based on your own criteria and—in the final chapter—have given you some guiding questions to help you in the process.

Our selection criteria ended with six RIAs who, we believe, are India's best advisers. Their details are given below in alphabetical order of first name.

#	Name	Year of Firm Set-up	Website
1	Dilshad Billimoria	2001	www.dilzer.net
2	Harsh Roongta	2015*	www.feeonlyinvestmentadvisers.com
3	Lovaii Navlakhi	2001	www.immpl.com
4	Melvin Joseph	2010	www.finvin.in
5	Suresh Sadagopan	2004	www.ladder7.co.in
6	Vishal and Shalini Dhawan	2003	www.planahead.in

Interviews with these advisers form addendums to each chapter in this book, so there are six chapters and six interviews. The format of these interviews broadly covers the following areas: a) a brief introduction to the RIA with his qualifications, work

---

* Harsh Roongta set up Apnaloan.com in 2000 and got his SEBI RIA license in 2013. He set up FOIA in 2015.

experience and achievements; b) a journey into their lives and how they got around to setting up their practice, because I believe it's important for readers to know their adviser and his/her background; c) highlights and insights from the adviser's experience with his/her clients; and d) the adviser's views on the most commonly asked questions in personal finance: Where can I start learning about personal finance? Should I invest in stocks or mutual funds? Should I buy or rent a house? Which is better, passive or active investing? Are debt funds better than fixed deposits, and so on. Views on hot new topics like international investing and cryptocurrency are also covered.

As we finish this book, the last chapter contains specific tips that should help you in your journey in personal finance.

The six chapters carry interviews with six SEBI RIAs. The last chapter—prepared in collaboration with a seventh adviser—is full of checklists and two sample case studies to help plan for your goals. Financial advisory is a new and developing profession. SEBI introduced the Investment Adviser (IA) rules only in 2013. The RIAs in this book, however, have been entrenched in financial planning since the early 2000s and were among the first to get their SEBI RIA license. The interviews are rich with their insights and wisdom that are useful to all of us.

I suggest that you read the book in its entirety and come back for specific insights in each interview. You can develop your own calculators in MS Excel based on the calculators given in the final chapter. Learning is a continuous process, and I hope this book becomes a part of your journey.

1

A Brave New World

Everything changed in March 2020. In electrical wiring, a circuit breaker halts the flow of a surge in current to protect equipment from damage. In stock markets, a circuit breaker halts trading to protect the markets from surging or collapsing. Introduced by SEBI[1] in 2001, a circuit breaker is a rare event. So, when two lower circuits happened in the span of ten days in March 2020, it was for the first time in twelve years (Dasgupta, 2020). The COVID-19 pandemic had disrupted the world and the stock markets were reacting to uncertainty that they hadn't faced since the global financial crisis. What was unfolding on television and trading screens was something that a twenty-five-year-old hadn't seen since school.

Two Years of Transformation

By 2020, half of India's population was under twenty-five years old.[2] A large part of this young population was already warming up (Sanghvi, 2019) to mutual funds. The COVID-19 pandemic tilted the scales significantly. The financial year 2020–21 (or FY21, from 1 April 2020 to 31 March 2021) broke

many records in the investing world, and the trend continued in
FY22. Consider the following data points:

1. Surge in New Accounts with Brokers

- By March 2021, the stock market had seen an
  unprecedented inflow of first-time investors. In an article
  (*Economic Times*, 2021), Ravi Kumar, CEO of brokerage
  Upstox, told Press Trust of India (PTI), 'Our customer
  onboarding surged over three times in FY21, adding
  more than 2 million, taking our customer base to over
  4 million. Of this, over 80 per cent are in the 18-36 age
  bracket, and over 70 per cent of the [sic] our customers
  are first-time investors.'
- In its FY21 annual report, leading brokerage ICICI
  Securities stated,[3] 'During the year, we had our best ever
  retail client addition of ~0.7 million and a total retail client
  base of ~5.4 million with over 1.91 million active clients
  and over 1.58 million NSE active clients. More than half
  of the new customers were below 30 years of age and about
  two-thirds are from Tier-II and Tier-III cities.'
- In a post titled 'Broking Goes Mainstream' on its blog,
  Zerodha stated,[4] 'It took us almost ten years to get to
  2 million customers, which was around the time COVID
  hit, and then we added our next ~6 million customers in
  just 18 months. Just for added context, we added 400,000
  customers in October 2021, while it took us seven years to
  add our first 400,000.'

2. Demat Accounts: Records Broken

- In FY21, the number of new dematerialized (Demat)
  accounts that were opened hit a record (Sultana &

Ramarathinam, *Mint*, 2021) of 14.2 million or more than thrice that of FY20 (4.9 million).

- The trend seen in FY21 wasn't a flash in the pan. It continued in the next financial year as well. The Ministry of Finance quoted[5] SEBI data that showed that India's Demat account holders more than doubled in three years to 7.38 crore (73.8 million) in October 2021. In seven months of FY22 (April 2021 to October 2021), the increase in the number of Demat accounts opened hit 18.7 million—which was more than the entire FY21 addition of 14.2 million.

3. Initial Public Offerings (IPOs): Surging Ahead

The new brokerage and Demat accounts opened in the past two years are also ferociously being used. In its January 2022 monthly bulletin,[6] SEBI chairman Ajay Tyagi gave the following data points:

- In just eight months (April 2021 to November 2021), the IPO proceeds (Rs 900 billion) almost trebled, compared to the level for the previous whole year (Rs 300 billion).
- The average size of IPOs has also grown to about Rs 12 billion in this financial year (FY22) from about Rs 3.5 billion during 2019–20.
- Up to November 2021 in 2021–22, the number of applications from retail individual investors in equity IPOs numbered 54.3 million, compared to 38 million in FY21 and only 7.7 million applications in FY20.
- The average number of applications in retail category per IPO on the Main Board rose to 1.56 million in FY22 (till November 2021) from 1.36 million in FY21 and 0.7 million in FY20.

• Investment by retail individual investors in IPOs has grown to Rs 151 billion till November 2021, from Rs 83 billion in FY21 and Rs 50 billion in FY20.

4. Mutual Fund Activity Picks up Pace

• In 2021, the Association of Mutual Funds of India (AMFI), reported[7] a sharp increase in folios (or mutual fund accounts—so one person can have multiple folios too) to 120.2 million folios as of December end 2021, from 94.3 million as of December end 2020. Thus, in one year, the industry added 26 million folios, compared to a total of 28 million folios that were added in the previous three years.

• While stocks and Demat accounts surged during FY21, AMFI data showed[8] that mutual fund (MF) Systematic Investment Plans (SIP) were sluggish. Monthly SIP contributions fell to Rs 73 billion in November 2020 from Rs 86 billion in March 2020. But this was followed by a sharp rebound as SIP collections touched an all-time high of Rs 113 billion in December 2021. The number of outstanding SIP accounts also steadily improved in FY22 to 49 million in December 2021 from 38 million in April 2021—an addition of 11 million accounts in nine months.

• 2021 was also one of the best years (Kripalani, 2021) for the mutual fund industry in terms of responses to new fund offers (NFOs), with collections (Rs 787 billion from April 2021 to November 2021 versus Rs 1.3 trillion in 2018) at the second highest in seven years. State Bank of India Mutual Fund's balanced advantage fund collected Rs 145 billion—the largest-ever (Moneycontrol, 2021) amount for a mutual fund offering.

5. Retail Participation in Equities Rises

- The Economic Survey for the year FY22[9] noted the increase in participation by individual investors in the equity cash segment driven by the rise in Demat accounts, and the rise in share of individual investors in total turnover at NSE, as given in the table below.

Share of Individual Investors in Equity Cash Segment Turnover (NSE) (in Per Cent)

Year	Share of Individual Investors
2016–17	36.0
2017–18	39.0
2018–19	39.0
2019–20	38.8
2020–21	45.0
April–October 2021	44.7

Source: SEBI (taken from Table 11, para 4.40, page 141 in Economic Survey 2022)

Investors today, including the large base of new ones that entered in the past two years, have a much wider pool of investment products to choose from than ever before. Options such as real estate investment trusts (REITs) and infrastructure investment trusts (InvITs) and debt exchange traded funds (such as the Bharat Bond) meant for institutional investors are also available to retail investors at low ticket size. Passive investing has picked up in a big way, aided by the decision (*Economic Times*, 2015) by the Employees Provident Fund Organisation in 2015 to invest in the stock markets. Thanks to the EPFO's investments, the SBI Nifty Exchange Traded Fund (ETF), with assets under management of Rs 1.2 trillion as of 31 December 2021,[10] is India's largest equity ETF.

Investments outside India (such as equity shares, ETFs, etc., in the USA) have also picked up, although this area is not as regulated as investing in the domestic market. The Reserve Bank of India's (RBI) Liberalized Remittance Scheme (LRS) was introduced[11] in 2004 with a limit of US$25,000, and through the years, this limit has been controlled by the RBI. In June 2015, the RBI increased the limit to US$250,000 from US$125,000 and between 1 Jan 2017 and September 2021, Indians wired out (Keshavdev, 2021) a record high US$68 billion. Although the large heads of expenditure within this amount include travel and education, many fintech apps (such as Winvesta, Vested, Stockal, etc.) now make investing directly in overseas stocks easy for Indian users. This was particularly useful in 2020 and 2021 when the group of stocks known as FAANG (Meta, formerly Facebook, Amazon, Apple, Netflix and Alphabet/Google) came into the limelight.

The Explosion in Equities, Explained

What drove this profound shift towards equities in India? There are two trends—short term and long term. In the short term, the pandemic-induced lockdown pushed many people locked up at home into the stock markets. In the US, major online brokers saw a spike in new accounts (Fitzgerald, 2020) in the first quarter (January–March 2020), driven by young and inexperienced investors. A similar pattern played out in India. As this Bloomberg article noted (Balwani, Mazumdar & Acharya, 2021):

As in other parts of the world, India's retail trading boom has been fueled by pandemic-driven restrictions and job losses that left millions of people at home with little to do. The relentless stock market rally since March 2020 has drawn in more investors. And technology, including the rise of cheap trading apps and social media—YouTube influencers, Twitter, and Telegram stock-tipping chat groups—has attracted hordes of day traders into discount brokers such as Zerodha Broking Ltd.

Every bull run is marked by excesses and one of the hallmarks of the 2020–2021 bull market was meme stocks. In the USA, as is well documented, the surge in retail investors into the stock market caused epic disruptions in the prices of some stocks, known as meme stocks, or stocks propelled by online communities. Even before the pandemic hit with full force, the famous r/WSB (r/WallStreetBets) subreddit was gathering momentum (Kawa, 2020). The pandemic, however, saw an all-out battle between r/WSB and mainstream Wall Street. At its peak, r/WSB and other online communities forced larger, institutional investors to sit up and take notice. In January 2021, the *Wall Street Journal* reported (Banerji, Chung & McCabe, 2021):

> The newbie investors are gathering on platforms such as Reddit, Discord, Facebook and Twitter. They are encouraging each other to pile into stocks, bragging about their gains and, at times, intentionally banding together to intensify losses among professional traders, who protest that social-media hordes are conspiring to move stock prices.

Online communities on stocks and investing were always active in India, with forums such as Valuepickr, blogs like *Alpha Ideas*, and message boards on portals like Moneycontrol. But the pandemic saw a new breed of investors hungry to know more. India has its own version of r/WSB called r/dalalstreetbets, which is much smaller at 10,600 members (as of 16 May 2022), compared to r/WSB's size of 12.1 million 'degenerates' (as they call themselves[12]). However, the r/IndiaInvestments subreddit is much bigger, with more than 156K members (as of 16 May 2022) and a wide range of topics for beginners to learn from. There are also communities on apps such as Slack, Discord, WhatsApp and Telegram; and this is over and above the discussions on social media platforms such as Twitter. So powerful is the interest in equities that an entire ecosystem of websites, apps and forums has developed providing free research and analysis. Influencers on Twitter post lengthy threads on stock ideas, fundamental analysis and much more. In early 2021, live audio community platform Clubhouse became popular (Mandavia, 2021) in India, providing another avenue for communities to discuss stocks and personal finance. Twitter also started its own live audio service called Spaces, where major events like the Union Budget as well as big moves in the stock market are discussed regularly with large audiences listening in.

The noise and drama of 2020 and 2021 have worn out in early 2022 in the USA. The rush of the stock markets is wearing thin as the worst of the pandemic seems to be over and people return to work. Stay-at-home stocks saw their prices correct (Wittenstein, Turner & Bloomberg, 2022) in January 2022 and GameStop—the meme stock at the centre of the battle between r/WSB and Wall Street—started (Gonsalez, 2022) the year at a stock price of US$19, much lower than the record high of US$483 back on 28 January 2021. The Russia–Ukraine war and the advent of an era of higher interest rates have impacted stock markets globally. In India, retail investor interest remains buoyant despite the steep correction in the stock market, with the number of SIP accounts hitting a record high (Dhawan, 2022) of 5.39 crore in April 2022. The shift in India's investment behaviour, thus, seems more enduring and to understand that, we need to understand the longer-term story.

The Inexorable Move to Financial from Physical Assets

Zoom out from the past two years and you will notice a major shift, better known as the 'financialization of savings', which had started even before the pandemic struck in India. A July 2017 RBI report (RBI, 2017) on Indian household finance by the Household Financial Committee noted the following breakup of assets held by the Indian household:

Asset	% of Total Assets	Description
Real estate	77	residential buildings, buildings used for farm and non-farm activities, constructions such as recreational facilities, and rural and urban land
Durable goods	7	transportation vehicles, livestock and poultry, agricultural machinery and non-farm business equipment
Gold	11	
Financial assets	5	deposits and savings accounts, publicly traded shares, mutual funds, life insurance and retirement accounts
Total	100	

More importantly, the RBI study found that the average Indian household tends to borrow later in life and goes into retirement with debt to be repaid—a precarious financial position in retired life where there is no steady recurring income. Making a strong case for moving towards financial assets, the RBI noted:

> If households in the middle third of the gold holdings distribution re-allocated a quarter of their existing gold holdings to financial assets, on average, they could earn an amount equivalent to 0.8% of their annual income per year (on an ongoing flow basis). Expressed differently, the wealth gain in real present value terms accruing from this shift would be sufficient to move these households roughly 1 percentage point (pp) up the current Indian wealth distribution.

To bring banking to the unbanked and raise financial inclusion at a mass scale, the Indian government introduced the Jan Dhan programme in August 2014. The demonetization of old currency notes of Rs 500 and Rs 1000 in November 2016 led to a significant 48 per cent increase (Singh & Roy, 2017) in Pradhan Mantri Jan Dhan Yojana accounts, with 18 million accounts being added from 9 November 2016 to 25 January 2017. Demonetization also drove significant flows to mutual funds. As the RBI noted (Dash, Singh, Herwadkar & Behera, 2017), 'An important positive impact of demonetization has been to induce a shift towards formal channels of savings by households. During demonetization and the subsequent period, there has been a distinct increase in savings flows into equity/debt oriented mutual funds and life insurance policies.'

While demonetization might have pushed people to invest in mutual funds, the financialization of savings in India is a much bigger shift, which impacted small savings schemes as well, showing the depth of penetration of financial products. Data analytics firm IndiaDataHub noted,[13] 'Cumulative inflows (under small savings schemes) in the last six years (FY17–22RE) have been ₹14 trillion (or approx. $200 billion at the current exchange rate)! In contrast, in the preceding six years (FY11–16), inflows were a modest ₹2.9 trillion (or approx. $38 billion at the current exchange rate) . . . Net collections under small savings between FY19–21 are almost 2x the net collections by the various MF (mutual fund) schemes.'

Beyond new bank accounts and small savings schemes, the biggest beneficiary of the financialization of savings are mutual funds. Mutual fund assets under management doubled[14] to Rs 38 trillion in January 2022 from Rs 17 trillion in January 2017 in five years. A mass-market ad campaign helped the industry along the way. In 2017—admittedly a bull market year with the Nifty up 29 per cent (31 December 2017 over 31 December 2016)—the AMFI launched (*Economic Times*, 2017) its famous 'Mutual Funds Sahi Hai' investor awareness outreach campaign. Spearheaded by AMFI and funded by mutual funds out of an investor education fund, the ad campaign was launched across media channels such as television, digital, radio, print, cinema and outdoor hoardings. Using the biggest mass sports in India—cricket— AMFI signed up as an associate sponsor of IPL 2020 and roped in (*Economic Times*, 2020) high-profile cricketers such as Sachin Tendulkar, Mithali Raj and M.S. Dhoni as part of the campaign.

Thus, while the pandemic pushed a new breed of investors into the stock markets, at a broader level the gradual shift towards financial products was already playing out across households in India. This shift will continue to play out as widening financial inclusion and the resultant increase in awareness of investment products spread across India. The journey has only begun. In the next chapter, I give the background of India's journey in financial products and then examine how fintech start-ups have disrupted the way we save and invest. I then outline the opportunity ahead for India's economic growth and how you can secure your financial dreams. The final two chapters will help you start the journey to achieve your dreams and checklists to get you started today.

Adviser Perspectives: Dilshad Billimoria

SEBI registration number: INA200002239
Website: https://www.dilzer.net/

Introduction

Dilshad Billimoria is managing director of Dilzer Consultants, based in Bengaluru. Dilzer Consultants was set up in July 2001 and currently has more than 450 clients across the globe. Dilshad has a bachelor's degree in business management from the University of Bangalore and has undergone extensive training in financial planning: she is a Life Underwriting Training Fellow from LUTCF, USA, holds a certificate in financial planning (CFP) from FPSB India and completed her foundation course in financial life planning from the Kinder Institute of Life Planning. Dilshad is active in the financial planning industry in India and is a director at the Association of RIAs (ARIA). Just 10 per cent of SEBI RIAs are (Koppikar, 2020) women and Dilshad is among this very slim percentage. I spoke with Dilshad on 5 October 2021, and these are the highlights of my conversation.

It took just two years from graduation day for Dilshad to start her financial planning firm, Dilzer Consultants, in 2001.

'This was an exciting leap of faith for someone who wanted to study hotel management. Like any other person at the cusp of starting her graduation, I had no idea what to do! I was planning to pursue hotel management, but a career-counselling session revealed that I had a flair for numbers and talking with people and that was when I decided to do a graduate degree in business management,' she told me. Dilshad credits her father for these critical decisions early in her life. She adds, 'The decision to start my firm also came from my father. He knew that I couldn't work under anyone else, and I needed to be on my own.'

After working in business development at the Aditya Birla Sunlife Group for just two and a half years, Dilshad started her firm with just two clients she acquired from her previous job. 'In the beginning, we were mainly distributors of financial products. 2008 was a turning point when I cleared the exams for the certified financial planner (CFP) exams from FPSB India. After getting the CFP certification, I shifted my focus towards financial planning. I realized that at the end of the day, if I'm able to solve a problem for a client as if it were my problem, that would give me a lot of satisfaction. Eventually, problem-solving became second nature. Even today, most of my business is via referrals,' she told me.

Looking back at her progress, Dilshad has only two regrets—first, that she should have done her post-graduation early on for a formal learning programme, which would better her domain expertise (she is now pursuing her MBA to meet SEBI RIA requirements), and second, that she should have taken on a business partner while starting Dilzer. While Dilshad's husband heads the IT function at Dilzer, he is a professional corporate trainer in information technology by profession.

Dilshad is among the very few women RIAs in India, and I asked her if this was a hurdle in her career. 'I never really felt it challenging to be a woman financial adviser; it worked in my favour. I never felt like I'm competing with men. There's a place for everybody, given that there are many people who genuinely need good advice. Even when I look at people who've done more business than me in half as many years, I don't have any regrets. Maybe I could have had a more goal-oriented focus. Still, I get a good night's sleep and the satisfaction of knowing that every recommendation that I make is backed by research and there is no dilution in what we give to our clients both in advice and in service delivery,' she told me. Dilshad had an all-women team when she started Dilzer, and even today, six of her thirteen employees are women. 'It was fantastic to build an all-women team. COVID-19 has forced WFH (work from home), but our team has been doing it for a long time. I felt that a woman working has more efficiency, more accountability, responsibility and honesty. They have more empathy and better listening skills. I do not mean this as a stereotype. I'm not making a feminist statement. Still, I have seen this in my experience—some of our male clients have opened out (financial and personal) to our women planners in a way they wouldn't have done to their wives or to male financial planners. That is what I have seen in my experience thus far.

Men, Women and Money

Are women and men different when it comes to money? 'Men are hunters, so they are always finding the best returns and they look only at the bottom line. Men look for the returns, women look for the process. One question that I get asked from male clients and never from female clients is—how you would rate me among all your clients? So, I have to explain to them that there is no rating in financial planning because each client's needs and situations are different,' she told me.

As we delve further into the topic of financial planning and women, I asked Dilshad what would be her advice on financial planning for a twenty-five-year-old woman starting her career? 'We begin our financial plans with an open talk and discuss needs, problems and objectives that we are trying to address. We insist on some non-negotiable goals such as an emergency corpus, life insurance and health insurance. Other than that, we have certain guidelines such as keeping debt below 30–35 per cent of total assets, keeping your cashflows free of commitments to low-yielding investments like cashback plans, endowment policies, etc.,' she explained to me.

I asked Dilshad how financial planning is different for women. 'Our female clients come from diverse backgrounds— single, married, divorced, widowed, married and working or homemakers,' she explained.

'Of these, the widowed and the divorced categories show the biggest change in behaviour from when they were married. For example, they now want to know much more about what they are investing in. They do their own research on recommendations that we make to them—and I think this is probably because they've had a bad experience in the past and are learning from their mistakes. In some extreme cases, we've seen women who are grieving the loss of a loved one change their adviser for no perceptible reason. So, everything in their lives was moving along just fine, and then suddenly, the loss of a loved one came as a big shock. So, divorced and widowed women are two categories that are the most unpredictable in terms of behaviour as compared to their married counterparts.'

Among married women, there is a difference in the behaviour of working women and homemakers. 'Working women are more in charge of their (family) finances than their male counterparts. Working women are hands-on and rectify problems when they see them, for example, when cash flows are too tight, when debt ratios are too high, etc., they go to the extent of reducing costs or compromising on goals. They ensure that our recommendations are complied with,' Dilshad told me.

Homemakers, however, are different. 'For a long time, homemakers didn't attend our financial planning meetings because (as per them) they didn't understand finance. In some cases, their husbands would tell them not to go for fear of asking the wrong questions. So, we put our foot down and insisted that both spouses attend our meetings. No question is bad, no question is stupid, and no question is wrong. Sometimes the best and most practical solutions come from homemakers. Being a woman, I work closely with them, for example, helping them create their own financial goals. We explain the benefits of financial literacy and becoming independent, and increasingly, we are seeing this (learning about money and finance) gaining ground,' she said.

How to Choose a Financial Adviser

Choosing the right adviser is an important decision, especially because this is your adviser for life. I asked Dilshad what basic questions and criteria we should look at while shortlisting and choosing advisers. 'Experience, certification and fiduciary responsibility,' summed up Dilshad. By experience, she meant the number of years of experience that the planner has in her advisory practice. Certification is important for the client to know because as per SEBI, only RIAs can provide investment advice. And finally, fiduciary responsibility means putting the client's interests above her own.

Adviser qualifications can get confusing for people who are not well versed with financial terms. 'I wouldn't recommend someone to blindly trust an adviser just because he or she has an RIA licence. Some mutual fund distributors are also as good as

RIAs but may not have switched to an RIA model for various reasons. Ultimately, it's about ethics and the way an adviser deals with clients. That's why further checks should be done by clients looking for advisers. Advisers have trial periods so clients can use that for seeing if they can work well with them,' she told me.

So, where can a novice start to learn about money? With a wry smile, Dilshad told me that younger millennials who approach her think they know more than her and she lets them discover things on their own before they turn to her. For people who want to DIY, Dilshad recommends a mix of simple products, such as provident fund (PF: for tax benefits) and ELSS (equity-linked saving schemes: for asset allocation), as starting points.

Range of Financial Products and Recommendations

What are the basic, essential, primary financial products that we should own? Dilshad adds mutual funds to life and health insurance that she mentioned earlier in the interview. Her firm offers model portfolios for each client (as per their risk profile). While Dilshad has a separate division for stock advisory, she recommends mutual funds for new clients who haven't invested in funds before, simply because it covers the entire gamut of investment objectives needed to meet goals.

What are products that she recommends to her clients? 'We are a one-stop shop for products and services. So, insurance, mutual funds, provident fund (PF), equity-linked savings schemes (ELSS), gold (in the form of sovereign gold bonds), portfolio management schemes (PMS), alternate investment funds (AIF), real estate investment trusts (REITs), private equity and international investing are some investment products that we recommend to our clients,' she told me. All portfolio recommendations are reviewed and updated regularly and then discussed via our financial planners to ensure that we maintain high-quality advice and alignment with client goals. Each time a client's decision differs from her firm's recommendations, this departure is recorded as part of client records. Dilshad follows a core and satellite construction in her recommendations. A core portfolio forms the bulk of investments and smaller allocations (satellites) are made around the core. So, the core allocation would consist of an index fund and flexi-cap or large-cap mutual funds. Depending on the risk profile and asset allocation requirements, the satellites would be towards sectoral, thematic, mid/small-cap allocations.

Rent or Buy a House? Invest in FDs or Bonds?

Buy or rent your home? Dilshad chuckles and admits it's a tricky question. 'If you do the math and if you're young, you'll go for rent especially if you are looking for experiential living, changing homes often and looking at short-term goals. Advisers like us, who have a more traditional mindset, believe in owning a roof over your head. But there is no strict rule, and everything depends on the unique client situation and their needs. Our job as advisers is to present the emotional and factual side of this debate,' she told me.

Fixed deposits versus debt funds? 'We show our clients post-tax returns on both FDs and debt funds. But within debt funds, none of our clients are below AAA-rated paper and ratings are monitored so that we switch out in case of downgrades. In case of FDs, we recommend Foreign Currency Non-Resident (FCNR) FDs to NRIs since the return on some of these are better than FDs.'

New Investment Areas

Finally, on new areas of investment, Dilshad does not advise
investment in cryptocurrencies since this is an unregulated
investment space. Her preferred mode of international
investment is via fund of funds and equity shares listed overseas.
'Many clients in the USA should not miss out on the currency
rate (INR–USD) differential. And when these clients have forex
transactions, say, for business purposes, or for sending a child
for overseas studies, we recommend international investing via
direct equity or fund of funds depending on the client and her
requirements,' she tells me as we wrap up the interview.

2

Kal, Aaj Aur Kal

To understand where India is today, it's important to understand where we've come from. Today we take investing in shares of Apple, Facebook, Google, etc., for granted, whereas this was not even possible a few decades ago for a variety of reasons ranging from regulation to lack of customer-friendly technology. Opening a brokerage account, a bank account, or starting a mutual fund SIP—all of these can happen sitting at home, with your smartphone. We've indeed come a long way from standing in line (Adajania, 2013) to invest in the Morgan Stanley Growth Fund in 1994. Ideas of risk and return have evolved over decades from the stock market as a gambler's den to an SIP in an equity mutual fund being a serious tool for long-term wealth creation. This chapter gives some background on how investment products evolved in India and helps you understand the profound change that I describe in the next chapter.

Elon Musk famously tweeted,[1] 'Who controls the memes, controls the Universe.' Generation X-ers like me didn't have memes in our childhood to help us understand things better (or to make fun of things). So, I can understand how those of

21

my generation struggle to understand their kids who feed on memes day in, day out. Memes are a great sign of the generation gap that exists today between Generation X, Millennials and Generation Z (if you follow the Pew Centre). I recommend readers to go through Buzzfeed's list[2] of '41 Things That Are Just Too Damn Real If You Have Indian Parents' to understand this generation gap and to have a good laugh at some of the memes. One tweet reads,[3] 'Desi parents never actually bought new batteries for the TV remote. They'd just slap the shit out of it hoping it'd start working again and then blame u for watching too much TV.' So, if you don't have a good laugh or—worse—don't understand the meme, then you know which side of the gap you're on. Another way to understand this generation gap is to watch[4] the web series *Tech Conversations with My Dad*. Made by the brilliant The Viral Fever (TVF), the series is free to air and consists of short (under eight minutes) hilarious videos featuring a son (Jitendra Kumar) explaining technology to his father (Gajraj Rao).

Kids today are growing up with choices, whereas their parents grew up in an India with compulsions, and their grandparents in an impoverished India with severe constraints. A twenty-five-year-old working in the 1970s had to wait in line for years to get a scooter and a landline phone. A twenty-five-year-old working in the 1990s had to be careful about outstation calls and enjoyed a fuel-efficient four-stroke motorcycle. A twenty-five-year-old working in the 2020s has 1–2GB/day mobile data and can choose between an electric two-wheeler and, say, a stylish gearless scooter. Consumer choices apart, my generation (those born in the early 1970s) can understand their parents' obsession with buying a house to secure a roof over one's head and stick with the same job for most of their career. But today's generation believes in rent, the gig economy and taking career breaks. This attitude towards work and towards life changes the very idea of risk (in life and with investments) and return (in terms of expectations from life and from investments). So, generation gaps are stark for every generation but when it comes to money, this generation is more distant than the previous ones. Memes are just one way to gauge how wide this generation gap is today. But since this book is about personal finance and not pop culture, it's important for readers to know how financial products developed in India post Liberalization to appreciate the depth of change in products and attitudes in the past decade.

Describing the generation gap, Shalini Dhawan, a SEBI RIA whose interview is in Chapter 6 of this book, told me, 'We have clients where we work across three generations (grandparents, parents, children), so we can share some anecdotes. The senior (retired) generation has wealth but is still in wealth-preservation mode. Our planning and simulations show they are comfortable but when we tell them that they can enjoy and spend, they tell us that they'd rather leave that money for the next generation. The next generation (fifty-year-olds and above) are in a midlife crisis. After working hard for decades, they're wondering if they should plunge into entrepreneurship or explore an early retirement. They have many goals (taking care of their parents, taking care of their children) to be met so it's about what are the trade-offs they may have to do. The next generation (twenty-year-olds) is still exploring money. Unlike their parents or grandparents, these kids are not deprived of wealth. So, they've not faced the same situations as their previous two generations and—as planners— we help them balance their priorities. This is a new India that we're seeing, and it will be interesting to see how it evolves.'

Suresh Sadagopan, a SEBI RIA whose interview is in Chapter 5, told me, 'The generations before were literally living in a different age. In that time, the options were really limited. There were fixed deposits, bonds, small savings instruments and some basic insurance plans. And they were very attractive because interest rates were high in those days. When the returns were so good, there was no incentive to take risks unnecessarily into equities.' Let's take a few steps back in memory lane to see how stock markets and mutual funds evolved in India.

From Gambling Den to Long-Term Investment

India has the oldest stock exchange in Asia, with the Bombay Stock Exchange (BSE) formed[5] as the Native Share and Stock Brokers Association in 1875. But the cult of stock investing started more than a 100 years later with the famous Reliance Industries IPO in 1977. To give you an idea of the magnitude of Dhirubhai Ambani's impact on stock markets and the size of the equity cult that he created, read this extract from Hamish McDonald's book (McDonald, 2010), *Ambani and Sons*:

> Between 1980 and 1985 the number of Indians owning shares increased from less than a million to four million. Among those, the number of shareholders in Reliance rose to more than a million by the end of 1985. It was by far the widest shareholder base of any Indian company—and, until the privatisation of major utilities like British Telecom or Nippon Telephone & Telegraph, probably in the world.

The success of RIL's IPO was despite, or probably because of, the Controller of Capital Issues (CCI) which was finally repealed in 1992, to give way to the Securities and Exchange Board of India (SEBI). Since the CCI under-priced public issues to favour investors, stock prices were vulnerable to manipulation by market operators, often in connivance with company promoters. In his book (Chikermane, 2018), *Seventy*

Policies That Shaped India: 1947 to 2017, Independence to $2.5 Trillion, Gautam Chikermane wrote, 'The control over the amount as well as its pricing converted the office of CCI into a zero-risk, high return lottery-ticket dispenser, as the prices of the shares offered to the public through capital markets were tremendously undervalued, giving a huge margin to investors and speculators on listing.'

From the mid-1980s to late-1990s, banks offered more than 10 per cent on deposits of more than five years. In FY1995–96, rates were as high as 13 per cent[6]—which meant that you could double your money in just over five years. With such high rates, the volatility of equity stocks made them an inferior option. Recalling the days when equities paled in comparison to company fixed deposits which yielded 13–14 per cent, markets veteran R. Balakrishnan wrote (Balakrishnan, 2022):

> With this kind of returns on debt investments, it is no wonder that equity investments were simply not on the radar of most ordinary investors. The shallow stock market with its extremely high transaction costs, zero transparency and a paperwork-laden system wasn't attractive to most, especially as income levels were also poor, making for poor risk appetite. Buying and selling stocks was not very easy and awareness about wealth creation through the stock markets had not yet set in. Fixed income apart, gold and real estate were the most preferred avenues to channelize investment.

Interest rates were eventually deregulated by the RBI as part of broader financial sector reforms. Some of these reforms were also ushered in thanks to recurring scams in the stock market. Economists Ajay Shah and Susan Thomas of the Indian Council for Research on International Economic

Relations (ICRIER) wrote a working paper in December 2002 titled 'The Evolution of the Securities Markets in India in the 1990s'. This summary given below of a list of scams in the 1990s is taken from this paper:[7]

Year	Event	Amount
1992	Harshad Mehta scam involving both GOI bonds and equity markets	Rs 54 bn
1994	MS Shoes share price manipulation and broker default	Rs 170 mn
1995	Sesa Goa share price manipulation and margin failure by brokers	Rs 45 mn
1995	Rupangi Impex (RIL) and Madan Industries (MIL) share prices manipulation	Rs 11 mn (RIL), Rs 5.8 mn (MIL)
1995	Bad deliveries of physical certificates	-
1997	Market manipulation by the CRB (CR Bhansali) Group	Rs 7 bn
1998	BPL, Videocon and Sterlite: share price manipulation	Rs 0.77 bn
2001	Ketan Parekh scam and leveraged positions in 'K10 stocks'	-

Source: Ajay Shah and Susan Thomas, 'The Evolution of the Securities Markets in India in the 1990s', page 8, download link in endnotes

So, if you find the older generation referring to the stock market as a gambler's den, you know where they're coming from. The 1990s saw a profound and fundamental shift in market regulation with the following changes (Shah & Thomas, 2002):

Year	Reform	Description
1994	Electronic trading	All exchanges in India switched from floor trading to anonymous electronic trading.
1996	Risk containment at the clearing corporation	The largest exchange, NSE, adopted risk management through 'novation' at the clearing corporation. Other exchanges also substantially improved their risk containment mechanisms.
1996	Dematerialization	Almost all equity settlement today takes place at the depository.
2000, 2001	Derivatives trading	In 2000 and 2001, equity derivatives trading commenced, with index derivatives and derivatives on some individual stocks.
2001	Elimination of leveraged trading on the spot market	'Futures style settlement' and deferral mechanisms, which implied that the spot market featured leverage and futures–market principles, were banned in favour of rolling settlement.

Source: Ajay Shah and Susan Thomas, 'The Evolution of the Securities Markets in India in the 1990s', page 7, download link in endnotes

If the tables given above seem too full of jargon, then read this pithy summary taken from a January 2022 post on LinkedIn[8] by banking veteran, and MD and CEO, SBFC Finance, Aseem Dhru. Recalling his days at HDFC Bank when dematerialization of shares was first introduced, Aseem wrote:

When we started lending against shares in #hdfcbank in 1997 shares were also in physical and most of you would not even know it now it used to come attached with a paper called the Transfer form and the seller would simply sign behind and deliver the shares to the buyer through a broker. In a year multiple such transfers would happen with no record—like a bearer bond. The form was valid for a year within which the buyer would have to send the certificate and transfer form to the registrar who in most cases would promptly return the shares as signature mismatch with their records. Now the circus began to trace the seller and get his signature done again hoping it would be right this time. Meanwhile all corporate actions like divided, bonus, right went to the seller.

Then came NSDL[9] and we opened demat accounts of our clients and sent all the shares in our vault for transfer unleashing chaos in the interim with certificates and transfer forms being returned and the bank running around to get them rectified. Institutional investors arrived on the scene only post demat and NSE taking off. Without transparency there can be no serious investments.

As stock markets became more transparent, so did corporate accounting standards. Listing agreements (between the stock exchanges and companies who want their shares listed on these exchanges) require companies to declare specific information regularly in the public domain. Far more data is available today to investors than there was in the 1990s or earlier. Reliance Industries' FY1976–77 annual report (still available on their website) was all of thirty-three pages, whereas their FY2020–21 annual report was 215 pages (admittedly the company today is also far more complex and diversified). Infosys's annual report for FY1993–94 was thirty-nine pages, whereas its FY2020–21 annual report was 320 pages. Thus, transparency and corporate governance standards today are more robust than in the previous generation. This does not mean that stock market scams or broker defaults have ceased completely; it means that the regulator and the market infrastructure today has evolved to become more shareholder-friendly and investor-focused than in the 1980s and 1990s.

The Rise of Mutual Funds

If Reliance Industries IPO in 1977 started the cult of equity investing in India, then mutual funds in the 1980s and 1990s were the first steps towards routing household savings into avenues other than fixed deposits, real estate and gold in India. Even though the first mutual fund in India was launched in the 1960s, the entry of private sector mutual funds in the 1990s widened the base. Here is the history of mutual funds in India as outlined by the Association of Mutual Funds of India (AMFI):

Years	Event	Examples	Mutual Fund Industry, Assets Under Management (AUM)
1964–1987	Unit Trust of India (UTI) formed in 1963.	US-64 launched	UTI: Rs 6700 crore (end-1988)
1987	Launch of public sector mutual funds by public sector banks.	Mutual funds from SBI, Canara Bank, Punjab National Bank, LIC, GIC, etc.	Rs 47,004 crore (end-1993)

Years	Event	Examples	Mutual Fund Industry, Assets Under Management (AUM)
1993–2003	Entry of private sector mutual funds	Kothari Pioneer, Morgan Stanley, Aditya Birla Sun Life, Templeton MF, and many more	Rs 1.2 lakh crore (end-Jan 2003)
2003–2014	UTI split into SUUTI and UTI Mutual Fund, mergers and acquisitions between mutual funds	Alliance Capital MF acquired by Birla Sun Life AMC, Sun F&C acquired by Principal, etc.[10]	Rs 6.1 lakh crore (31 December 2011)
2014–present	SEBI introduced progressive measures to increase penetration of mutual funds beyond metro cities	SEBI launched direct plans in 2013, SEBI rationalized mutual fund schemes in 2017[11]	Rs 37.7 lakh crore (31 December 2021)

Source: History of Mutual Funds in India, Association of Mutual Funds of India (AMFI) website

The Changed Face of Investment Advice

The evolution of companies, stock markets, regulators and mutual funds over the past three decades has been accompanied by a more recent evolution of the last mile in investing, namely the advisers. Through the 1980s and most of the 1990s, financial advisory was not a formally regulated profession. Investing in the stock markets was based on tips—from your bank manager, friends and family, colleagues, newspapers and TV media, or even advice from your friendly chartered accountant who filed your income tax returns. So, while the Reliance Industries IPO in 1977 created a huge base of retail investors, these investors became fair game to be taken for a ride. For example, just five years later, Reliance Industries shares were caught (Kaul, V., 2011) in the grip of a bear cartel attack that impacted investors and was unrelated to RIL's core business.

Investment frameworks, equity research methodologies and advice have developed alongside the capital markets in the past few decades. Today, there are many blogs where you can learn how to research stocks, there are tools to back-test strategies, and there are even websites like Smallcase that let you invest in a basket of stocks based on your investment thesis. None of this existed in the 1980s or 1990s. If you were serious about investing, your best bet was a group of like-minded people. ICICI Prudential chief investment officer, Sankaran Naren, often refers to a Chennai club that he was part of in the 1990s. Narrating how this club helped him evolve, Naren told (Mukherjea, Moneycontrol, 2018) Saurabh Mukherjea, 'It was very important because we had made a number of big investing mistakes in (19)94, (19)95. When the bear market arrived in (19)98, all our investing mistakes showed up clearly. What was interesting was you realize that you were not the only person making the mistakes and that there were many others who had made similar mistakes.' Today—as you will see in the next chapter—you can build a strong foundation to help you develop your investment framework and keep learning about personal finance, provided you curate your content consumption well.

The entry of private mutual funds in the 1990s provided an indirect way of investing in equities by trusting a fund manager with the expertise and resources to track the stock markets. Mutual funds also gave rise to the mutual fund distributor (MFD) who served the needs of the small investor in an analogue era—everything from helping to open mutual fund folios, taking care of documentation for transactions like purchase, redemption, SIPs, change in bank accounts, and much more. MFDs are paid by the mutual funds and hence do not charge anything from investors. MFDs helped expand the mutual fund industry in a big way. Being the feet on the street, MFDs helped small-ticket, retail investors who didn't have the time to track the markets to invest regularly into both equity and debt markets. As mutual funds became popular, and as investors became savvy, SEBI moved (Kaur, 2018) to reduce costs and improve transparency by first banning entry loads in 2009 and mandating mutual fund houses to launch 'direct plans' in 2013—which meant that investors transacted directly with the mutual fund instead of going via the MFD. Direct plans are offered typically at a lower net asset value (NAV) than regular plans (which were sold by MFDs) since direct plans have lower costs. Finally, in 2013, SEBI introduced the SEBI (Investment Advisers) Regulations 2013 to formally regulate the practice of investment advice. The six interviews that you read in this book are from some of India's most senior financial advisers, all of whom took the RIA licence in 2013.

Almost all of the regulation and evolution of the stock markets and mutual funds before the outbreak of the

COVID-19 pandemic happened at what now seems like a leisurely pace. As we see in the next chapter, the entry of fintech start-ups completely changed the nature of investing and of personal finance.

Adviser Perspectives: Harsh Roongta

SEBI registration number: INA000014836
Website: www.feeonlyia.com

Harsh is among the most respected names in personal finance in India. His weekly column, Truth Be Told (earlier known as Frankly Speaking), has featured in *Business Standard* every fortnight for more than a decade. After two stints at ICICI Limited (before its merger with ICICI Bank in 2001) back in the 1980s and 1990s, Harsh ran two start-ups—Apnaloan.com and Apnapaisa.com. He exited Apnapaisa.com in 2015 to set up Fee Only Investment Advisers LLP (FOIA). FOIA offers the entire range of financial planning services, including comprehensive financial planning, tax advisory, NRI tax and remittance advisory services, investment management, etc. FOIA is based in Mumbai and their fees and contact details are available on their website given above. We had an almost-two-hour-long Zoom call on 2 October 2021 for the purposes of this chapter.

Harsh is a serial entrepreneur and has done many switches and pivots, so he understands how career transitions work and their impact on our finances and lives. A Mumbaikar from an early age, Harsh is a chartered accountant and comes from a family of highly educated professionals. To that extent, his decision to become an entrepreneur instead of settling down at ICICI Bank for a long career in banking seems counterintuitive. Harsh first joined the erstwhile ICICI Limited (which was merged with ICICI Bank in 2001) as an associate in 1985 in the leasing and investment banking divisions. He quit in 1990 to start a boutique investment banking firm with a few of his ICICI colleagues, who quit along with him and rejoined ICICI in 1998. 'K.V. Kamath (then MD and CEO of ICICI) was calling back some of the old employees and I decided to return. Whatever I am today is because of the mentorship I received and things I learnt at ICICI and from Kamath Sir,' Harsh told me.

At the erstwhile ICICI Limited, Harsh was among the early leadership team that built and developed the retail lending business. 'It was literally a start-up. There were lots of constraints, including constraints on salaries that we could pay to recruits, but we had complete freedom to build the product. I oversaw recruiting and the team we recruited back then is doing great things today,' recalled Harsh. However, this stint at ICICI would be his final one and in 2000, Harsh started Apnaloan.com at a time when India's retail lending business boom was taking off. However, as competitive pressures rose and costs mounted, Harsh wound down the business in 2005 and after two years of independent consulting, he started Apnapaisa.com which was similar to Apnaloan.com but without the loan fulfilment part. 'At that time (2007), loan fulfilment was the biggest cost so we cut that out and gave the (loan) leads to others to fulfil,' Harsh told me. After eight years, Harsh exited Apnapaisa.com by merging it with Andromeda and set up FOIA.

While FOIA started in 2015, Harsh's experience in advisory is much deeper. When I asked him how he built a financial planning practice with no experience in, say, mutual funds, Harsh told me, 'A lot of it is fortuitous. Unlike Apnaloan. com, Apnapaisa.com was broader and included insurance and mutual funds too. Alongside this, my newspaper column gave me mind share and that, coupled with my media appearances, gave me access to mutual fund industry CEOs. Technologies like WhatsApp allowed me to circulate my views to a broader audience. That's how I stayed in touch with industry veterans.' When I asked him what his biggest learnings from his entrepreneurial forays were, Harsh said, 'Everything is a people's business. What kept me awake at night was finding and retaining talent; and what worked for me is what I learnt at ICICI—throw people in at the deep end and tell them to swim. People step up, and they perform despite constraints.' Harsh's extensive knowledge in taxation coupled with the 'human capital' he developed while training under the likes of K.V. Kamath, Lalita Gupte and Shikha Sharma at ICICI helped him understand human behaviour in general and employee behaviour in specific. It is this knowledge that helps him understand his clients better at FOIA. His experience of career transitions in life helps him connect with clients at similar junctures in their lives.

At FOIA, Harsh focuses on middle- to senior-level corporate employees as well as entrepreneurs and professionals who run their own practice. Harsh loves the transparency that the SEBI RIA model offers. 'I became sick and tired of commissions which are an easy way of running a business because your income comes from the manufacturer (mutual funds, etc.) and your client is not paying you. But over the years, the market has evolved to understanding the importance and value of services based on transparent fees—and this understanding is only increasing. So now the client pays you for the value of your advice. This gives me the freedom to choose my clients and not go after size (assets under advice). And our fee structure is transparent—it is on our website. People appreciate transparency.'

Harsh's clients come from the higher income brackets where, he feels, the need for financial planning is clearly recognized. This cohort, however, is not immune to doubts and mistakes when it comes to their money. Harsh believes that having insights into things that directly affect you is very tough. When I asked him for his observations, he told me, 'One blinding insight for me was that even rich people need validation. A friend shared all the details about his finances but insisted that he'd do his own investments. After many conversations, it turned out that he wanted to buy a luxury car that cost Rs 50 lakh but, despite having sufficient money, he was feeling guilty about spending so much—so he wanted me to validate his decision! I've seen extremely smart people including fund managers who make strange decisions when it comes to their own money. One such fund manager's personal portfolio was full of endowment policies on the lure of "guaranteed returns". What he didn't realize was that the product was based on promised returns, not real returns,' Harsh told me.

'Another client got lucky with a property investment that increased in value after redevelopment. He asked me if he should sell this property. I asked him if he would buy the same property today if it was offered to him (at Rs 2 crore, the current market value) and he said he wouldn't. I told him that each day he held on to that property, it was costing him Rs 2 crore. That's when a lightbulb turned on in his mind. Most of our clients have that lightbulb moment while working with us, and it gives you a kick to be able to give that kind of blinding insight to some really smart people.'

Life-Planning Questions

Onboarding clients at FOIA is a detailed and lengthy process which includes structured questions to understand a client's risk appetite and his current status before aligning them to their financial goals. A client's expectations are central to the process and the structured questions help bring out what the client thinks. Some of these questions are life-planning questions designed by George Kinder:

- Imagine we begin working together and are having a meeting to mark the third anniversary of our relationship. And you are telling me, Harsh, you did a great job, and I am so glad that I decided to work with your firm. What would need to happen during these three years for you (the client) to feel like that?
- Imagine you win a lottery running into several crores (the amount changes depending on the client), and the money is in your bank account. This amount is more than sufficient to meet all your needs. Would you change anything in your life?
- Your doctor tells you that you have a terminal disease, and he has good news and bad news. The good news is that the disease will not affect your daily life. The bad news is that you have five to ten years left. What will you change in your life?
- You have twenty-four hours to live. What do you wish you had finished? What do you wish you had become? (Harsh always wanted to be a teacher.)

The answers to these questions give rich insights into the client and his family. 'We normally don't discuss returns in the onboarding process. I think these questions work because they focus on goals which are most important for them. It takes the focus away from expected returns to returns needed and the risk that will have to be taken for achieving that return,' Harsh told me. Harsh is not burdened by client expectations. Most clients come to him via referrals instead of him seeking business. 'This is a great starting point because I can ask the client what she is looking for instead of the client asking me what I can deliver. It helps me position my services with clients much better,' Harsh said.

Is It Important to Win the Race?

At FOIA, Harsh is a big fan of passive products. 'Asset allocation trumps the choice of security when it comes to returns from investments. All that an RIA does is asset allocation and ensure that the client follows through. Passive products are "fill it, shut it, forget it"—I don't need to think if I'm beating the market. All our plans have an "Enjoy Life Fund" where our clients can enjoy their money they make, instead of worrying about whether they are winning a race. It's too much work winning the race. The objective is to complete the race. If you (the client) are in it to win it, then maybe FOIA isn't the place for you,' he told me.

Some Common Yet Critical Questions

As we wrap up the conversation, I ask Harsh about transitions in life, and adverse events led by external and internal circumstances. 'The birth of a child, career changes and retirement are some of the biggest transitions we make in life. For one client, we helped him chart a two-year surplus before he left his job, and I was talking with him every day for a long time, handholding him through the process. Adverse events will keep happening, and these days they get compressed in time frames; you need to plan for contingencies. We do a lot of financial planning for disability, for death, we focus on wills, we tell clients to get insurance. We tell them to talk about uncomfortable things with their family—like, does your family know your views on the use of artificial life maintenance system like ventilators so that they can take a decision when you are not able to give them guidance?' Finally, I quiz Harsh on the most common questions that people ask in personal finance.

1. How do I choose passive investment products?

For index ETFs/index funds, we go by tracking errors at the NAV level and not at the closing price level. For example, the Nippon Nifty BeES ETF that we track has just a 0.8 per cent tracking error at the NAV level, but when tracked based on closing price, the tracking error increases to 2.5 per cent. For index funds, we do not look at AUMs, but at exit loads, funds with dividend and growth options (for stripping loss/profit), etc. We always prefer index funds over ETF for ease and certainty of dealing as well as liquidity provided due to the redemption option.

2. Should I buy or rent a house?

Once you've committed your life to a city, have the funds to make a down payment, if the EMI is not more than 30–35 per cent of income and you have a long-term view on your income, then you should buy a ready-to-move-in home. This is what I wrote in a 2015 *Forbes* article, 'I think these rent-versus-buy calculators miss a very significant cost, which is that of defying social convention. Buying your own house (even with a fat loan) is considered the sign of having achieved financial stability. The cost of social pressure is enormous and the sense of security you get by conforming to the social norm (of owning your own residence) is way too high to be ignored.'[1]

3. FDs or debt mutual funds?

FDs are terrible, lazy investments. Within debt funds, we may sometimes recommend period (duration) risk but never credit risk, so prefer, say, government securities for a longer-term duration when we are expecting interest rates to drop. We don't believe in recommending additional risk in debt products just to increase returns—we'd rather look at equities for increasing return.

4. Should I invest in new areas like international investing and crypto?

International investing should be part of asset allocation, even for retired people. India is less than 5 per cent of the world's GDP as well as market capitalization, so you need to have exposure to global investments; and now you have a great range of passive international products. We do not understand cryptocurrency and let clients use their discretionary 'mad money' allocation to invest in such products as per their desire. We do not charge fees on any investments made by the client from his 'mad money' allocation or in any investments made against our recommendations—this acts as an important remembrance tool for the client as to who took a particular decision.

5. What should I understand before making an investment/ purchase/financial decision?

Risk, return and liquidity. You should decide which is your objective function and which you should optimize. So, for a particular goal, if you have a targeted return, then you should ask yourself how you can achieve that return with the least compromise on risk and liquidity. For example, for a goal with a one-year horizon, liquidity is the most important factor irrespective of an individual's risk-taking ability and the investment choice needs to reflect that. A corpus for retirement that must last for 25–30 years should have a dash of equity even for the most conservative investor.

3

How Fintechs Changed Personal Finance

While technology has been transforming our lives for a long while now, the banking, financial services and insurance (BFSI) industry in India has seen a profound change in the past decade. Fintech start-ups have changed the way we bank, borrow, invest, lend, pay and save. Tailwinds of regulation, generous funding from venture capital, entrepreneurial spirit and the largesse of cheap mobile data are some of the factors that have driven the rise of fintech in India. As more people hopped on to apps, they became hungry to learn more about money. This hunger drove a boom in the way knowledge, advice and opinion gets disseminated. Today, from influencers to communities, everything is available at your fingertips. Not all of it is useful. This chapters looks at how all of this happened.

The Rise and Rise of Fintech in India

Technology disrupted finance many times over in the latter half of the past decade. Bank accounts, brokerage accounts, credit cards, mutual funds—some of the most important and basic financial products—can be opened in a matter of minutes, provided you have basic verification (KYC—Know Your Customer) in place. India's expansion of financial services has been so successful that the International Monetary Fund (IMF) wrote a paper[1] in February 2021 on how other emerging markets and developing economies can learn from our experience in building the now-famous digital infrastructure called the India Stack. Fintech is part of this transformation.

While there was no single magic moment or tipping point for fintech in India, one of the earliest predictions was back in 2015 by Nandan Nilekani, co-founder of Infosys and ex-chairman of the Unique Identification Authority of India (UIDAI). UIDAI developed the Aadhaar biometric system which is the 'A' in the JAM trinity (Jan Dhan–Aadhaar–Mobile), widely acknowledged as a pivotal driver for financial inclusion in India. Nilekani, while talking at an entrepreneurs' meet organized by The Indus Entrepreneurs (TiE), said, and I quote from an NDTV article:[2]

. . . in 2009 there was a WhatsApp movement in telecom. My analysis is, in 2015, there is a WhatsApp movement for finance in India.

Change is coming on many fronts . . . new licences, smartphone Aadhaar identification, e-sign, payment banks, etc. Some of it is regulated, some of it is technology, some of it is design, and some of it is market . . . [link to full video[3]]

Nilekani was right and change did come in a very big way. Paytm's digital wallet in 2014 was the first (*Mint*, 2019) Indian app to use a quick response (QR) code. It was such a runaway success that by December 2017, Paytm became the first Indian app to cross (Singh J., 2017) 100 million downloads. In April 2016, the Reserve Bank of India (RBI) launched the Unified Payment Interface (UPI) which went on to transform digital payments in India. In September 2016, Mukesh Ambani announced that Reliance Jio would offer free voice calls and unlimited data till 31 December 2016; Jio added 50 million subscribers in eighty-three days (Sengupta & Khan, 2016) and India is now the world's largest consumer of mobile data (Abbas, *Economic Times*, 2021). In November 2016, Prime Minister Narendra Modi announced demonetization of currency notes of Rs 1000 and Rs 500 denominations which would play a major role in spurring payments via digital platforms. All these seemingly unrelated events played a huge part in sparking the fintech revolution in India. Today, QR codes and UPI are the things we take for granted while making payments through our smartphones to just about anyone, from kirana shops to newspaper vendors. And the success is of a global scale. To put things in perspective, UPI crossed US$100 billion in value in December 2021 (Singh, T.D., 2022), just over five years after its launch.

Fintech sits right at the top of India's huge start-up ecosystem. The National Investment Promotion & Facilitation Agency's website[4] states that there are more than 2100 fintechs existing in India today, over 67 per cent of which have been set up in the last five years. The Indian fintech industry ecosystem consists of subsegments including Payments, Lending, Wealth Technology (WealthTech), Personal Finance Management, Insurance Technology (InsurTech), Regulation Technology (RegTech), etc. With the pandemic restricting our movement, everything went online. NASSCOM, India's apex body of the information technology and business process management (IT-BPM) industry, called 2021 'The Year of the Titans'. In its January 2022 report,[5] NASSCOM stated that BFSI (which includes fintech start-ups) in India enjoyed a lion's share of investments across all stages. In 2021, India added thirteen BFSI unicorns, and saw an increase in seed and late-stage median ticket size by four times, and had more than fifteen rounds of US$100 million-plus funding.

The best way to understand technology's impact on personal finance is to open your smartphone and check the number of personal finance apps. Almost every financial product in your life will have an app. So, you will have the apps of your banks (HDFC Bank, SBI, etc.), payments apps (like Paytm, Google Pay, etc.), investment apps (Smallcase, Paytm Money, ET Money, etc.), domestic stock market apps (Zerodha, Angel One, IIFL, etc.), international stock market apps (Winvesta, Vested, etc.), portfolio tracking apps (INDMoney, Mprofit, etc.) and so on and so forth. Even these are just scratching the surface because there are apps for lending, insurance, crypto and more. Payments are integrated within shopping apps such as Amazon, delivery apps such as Zomato, lifestyle apps such as Myntra, etc. So, you can now choose to pay via UPI, digital wallet, credit cards, and—one of the hottest fintech areas of the past few years—buy now pay later (BNPL). Thus, fintech start-ups in India have transformed financial habits in general and access to financial products in particular. For example, today, we can buy US stocks like Apple and Tesla sitting in our homes in India—all with the tap of an app. And people are lapping this up. In 2021, as per a *Times of India*[6] article (Hariharan, 2022), investments by Indians in the US stock markets more than doubled to US$300–500 million. Apps have enabled a change in saving habits, which can be seen in the ease of onboarding and starting an SIP in mutual funds. Starting an SIP is an easy and seamless process and, as mentioned earlier, SIP inflows in December 2021 crossed (Raj, 2022) Rs 11,000 crore—which is remarkable because SIP inflow was probably a rounding-off error in mutual funds flow a few decades ago. The sheer range of financial products now can be dizzying to anyone new to finance. And this is where technology played a role yet again—by creating a world of content to help us.

Welcome to the Influencer Economy

As access to financial products increased, so has advice. Today, on the Internet, there is free advice on almost everything, including money. And the people who influence your decisions are literally called influencers. In an exhaustive article on the influencer economy in India (pegged[7] at Rs 900 crore and growing at 25 per cent compounded annual growth rates), the Ken described (Khatri & Vishanathan, 2021) how influencers function:

> Highly capable of swaying people's decisions in real-time, influencers build up a personal brand that they can eventually monetise. If you're a brand selling, for instance, organic protein powder, chances are you'd get better traction if a popular fitness trainer offhandedly mentions it online rather than if you ran an old-fashioned TV advertisement.

The trend is even more prevalent in the USA where 'finfluencers' (or influencers in personal finance) routinely give investment tips to Gen Z, which is the generation following millennials or those born after 1997.[8] The impact of influencers was already known in fashion and lifestyle. The pandemic pushed them into finance as well. Describing a TikTok influencer, Bloomberg wrote (Egkolfopoulou, 2021):

> Influencers like Hankwitz can translate concepts like passive investing or tax harvesting into digestible social media videos using playful twists, music and colorful captions, making investment products and the like feel accessible to millennials and Gen Z-ers.

In hindsight, personal finance was ripe for demystification and simplification. Rather than read the onerous 'most important terms and conditions' that come with every credit card, millennials find it much easier to watch an influencer on YouTube or Instagram Reels tell you not to blow your spending limits. Financial products are full of jargon and are difficult to understand for most people. This is why these products have been sold by distributors and advisers who are trained in the profession. Unfortunately, the distribution channel tends to get paid by the industry which makes it tricky to trust them. But in the past decade, the rise of social media—fuelled by the pandemic-driven rush towards personal finance described in Chapter 1—drove the need for simplification of finance. And the influencer economy responded in full force. But popularity is easy, credibility is tough. Popularity can be built by creating the right content, but credibility comes with experience.

Learning, Old-School Style

Technology made blogging popular in the early 2000s. Blogging is a relatively old way of writing online, given that social media has moved the world to instant video or live short-form content (such as Twitter, YouTube, Instagram, etc.). But blogging is still very popular in the USA, where many investment firms (Collaborative Fund, Ritholtz Wealth) have widely read authors and their blogs. In India, there are comparatively fewer, credible and exhaustive personal finance blogs. One of the most credible people in personal finance, whom I have also hosted on my podcast, is Professor Pattabiraman (better known as Pattu). Pattu blogs at Freefincal.com, where he focuses mainly on retirement planning and has many calculators and downloadable excel sheets to help readers with their calculations.

But beyond retirement planning, Pattu also provides screeners for mutual funds and stocks, has a Nifty PE (price/

earnings) calculator and a robo adviser tool. Pattu's blog clearly states that it does not provide any individual investment advice. Pattu isn't your regular Instagram or YouTube influencer with stylish photos and catchy videos. He's a forty-six-year-old IIT Madras physics professor who learnt about money the hard way. Facing a medical emergency at home, Pattu went into debt and vowed never to revisit that situation again:

> At that time, I was also changing jobs, and was out of work and income for a few months. That was when I realised it was horrible to be in debt. There were so many things happening that I felt my life was not in control. First, I started learning how to get rid of my debt. The next was, how to never be in that situation again. (Santosh & Shah, 2021)

Pattu looks warily at fintech start-ups. 'The amount of disruptive innovation in this space is scary. It is a pity we still do not have proper privacy laws in place. Even if the data obtained is personally non-identifiable, I would prefer a simple paid service that neither sells my data to others nor uses it to upsell other products. As the saying goes, if something is offered for free, you are the product,' he told me. Pattu doesn't believe that this generation is unique when it comes to aspirations, knowledge and expectations around money and told me, 'I think most young people from *all* generations start out believing that there is a quick way to do something without discipline and toil; It is possible to get rich by returns alone with meagre income until life teaches them a thing or two!' Finally, when I asked him about the most common mistakes made by people in personal finance, he replied, 'Obsession about saving tax, buying real estate, not knowing where to draw the line for wants.'

The Power of Crowds

Online forums have also exploded in popularity, as described in Chapter 1. One of the most popular personal finance fora in India is the ASAN Ideas for Wealth Facebook Group (AIFW⁹). AIFW is moderated by Ashal Jauhari, a forty-four-year-old chemical engineer who works in Gandhidham, Gujarat. Ashal created AIFW in May 2011 and the group has more than 1,07,500 members. The group is buzzing with activity every day as members post their queries which are replied to by other members. There are strict rules on content (no business promotion is allowed, no discussion on crypto currencies, etc.) and Ashal spends a large part of his time (outside of his job) to ensure that discussions are conducted in a civil and polite manner. Ashal is very passionate about personal finance and goes out of his way to help people make the right decisions about their money. 'After having discussions with me, the wishes, the blessings, the goodwill, the trust, the respect, the love, the affection I receive from these people give me the satisfaction, the motivation to do more,' he told me.

Ashal agrees that the Internet has made knowledge more accessible. But that has come with a downside as well. 'Due to the spread of the Internet, knowledge is available in abundance. But if you ask me, there is less knowledge and more noise on the Internet. A very easily identifiable feature regarding today's young generation is instant gratification. Whether about small decisions or about serious goals like FIRE (financially independent, retired early—discussed in the next chapter), this generation wants to do it as soon as possible. This instant gratification or impulsive decision-making does more harm than good to their long-term financial habits,' he told me. Similarly, fintech start-ups have made things easier but they've also created another problem—the tendency to do something for the sake of it or to not miss out on a hot trend (better known as the fear of missing out, or FOMO). 'People can't sit idle on their portfolio; every now and then they want to buy, sell, switch, when there might not even be a need to do so. But people must think very hard before taking any action and ask themselves—is this (action) required at all?' The most discussed topics on AIFW were about which were the best mutual funds, the best insurance (health and life) and the best home loans. Members also discuss financial products such as savings plans (from insurance companies), tax-savings schemes, fixed deposits, etc. Some popular topics include behavioural finance (such as biases), taxation, equities (mental models, frameworks, etc.) and much more. Given that Ashal helps so many people with their personal finance problems, I asked him what the most common mistakes were that he encountered. Ashal listed them as under:

1. Not being able to say no to their near ones, even if they are aware that a product pushed by them is not good for their financial life.
2. Not purchasing adequate insurance, be it for life or for health or for any other assets and risks.
3. Not maintaining an emergency corpus.
4. On the pretext of avoiding volatility of equity, people happily chase returns on the fixed income side of their portfolio.
5. Either not investing in equity at all or investing too much into it.
6. People will first purchase a product and then try to link it with their needs and requirements. It should be the other way round.

Pattu, Ashal and Melvin Joseph (who is among the six advisers featured in this book) go back a long way. They, along with veterans in personal finance like trainer and educator P.V. Subramanya (of the *Subramoney Blog*), are active on AIFW and keep a close watch on the quality of content on the forum.

The Dark Side of Technology

Technology comes with its pitfalls. Investor behaviour and motivation—from greed to fear—don't change. But the sources of greed and fear have increased, thanks to the Internet. Where previously your friends/family would boast about their gains in the stock market, today, everyone posts their achievements on social media—from screenshots of stock trading gains to Instagram reels of lavish lifestyles earned from reward points. Social media and online fora are good at fuelling herd mentality, peer pressure and FOMO. In August 2019, YES Bank's stock price had corrected 85 per cent (Mehta, 2019) from its all-time high. Following this crash, Nithin Kamath of Zerodha wrote a post (Kamath, 2019) titled 'Lessons from Trading on Yes Bank', where he revealed that the number of Zerodha clients went up 8x in roughly the same period that the stock price crashed 85 per cent. Incidentally, YES Bank's stock currently (3 February 2022) trades[10] at around Rs 14, which is another 75 per cent down from the Rs 56/share in August 2019.

Talking about investment apps, Kayezad E. Adajania, head of personal finance at Moneycontrol.com, told me, 'I'm not a big fan of these apps. They're good to bring users in by the busload and they have an edge in areas such as ease in account opening and convenience in transactions. So, they're good for low-ticket transactions. But these apps are largely built with a technology bent of mind, not necessarily from a financial planner's mind frame. It's easy for the hottest funds in the market to be ranked, based on past performance—not necessarily the funds that are right for you. There's no guarantee these recommended funds will keep performing in the future.'

Bull markets are marked by exuberance, euphoria and excesses, and the rush into equities, during the pandemic, by newcomers was no different. Scamsters proliferated across messaging apps and online fora operating pump-and-dump schemes. Thanks to technology, the speed at which these scams operate can leave regulators like SEBI and RBI behind. While SEBI has warned investors to be cautious of these scams, in a bull market, these warnings get lost in the noise. In January 2022, veteran journalist Sucheta Dalal wrote a comprehensive article (Dalal, Moneylife, 2022) titled 'Many Ways of Being Fooled in a Bull Market', outlining these scams:

> On the contrary, hundreds of fraudulent tip-sheets and investment groups/channels are continuing to offer 'hot tips' and 'jackpot earnings' based on stories cooked up by self-styled experts and market operators. Each of them has thousands of subscribers. What makes them doubly dangerous is the use of paid influencers to give credibility to their false narratives and to aggressively discredit those who question or point to flaws in their theory.

As the article points out, half the investors are first-time investors in the stock markets, attracted by the bull run. Technology can enable us to make more informed decisions, but it can also overwhelm us with high-decibel noise and lead us to making bad decisions in the hunt for higher returns. Navigating a complex world can be tough for the under-prepared. How then should you prepare to achieve your financial dreams? The second half of this book will take you through the opportunity, and arm you with maps and plans to help you in your journey.

Adviser Perspectives: Lovaii Navlakhi

SEBI registration number: INA200010676
Website: www.immpl.com

Lovaii Navlakhi, founder and CEO at International Money Matters (IMMPL, a subsidiary of TVS Wealth), is an award-winning SEBI-registered investment adviser. Lovaii is among India's oldest and distinguished financial planners. His passion in financial planning is evident by the fact that he was in the first batch of certified financial planners (CFP) India in 2004 and the first certified financial transitionist (CeFT) in India in 2016. After working across large Indian organizations as well as a dot-com, Lovaii began IMMPL in 2001. Since then, he has worked with many clients and counts cross-border financial planning as his forte. In October 2016, TVS Capital acquired (Narasimhan, 2016) a majority stake in IMMPL. Lovaii is based in Bengaluru, and I spoke with him on 9 October 2021 for the purposes of this chapter.

Lovaii never set out to be an investment adviser. Educated in Mumbai, Lovaii is a Sydenham College alumnus and holds an MMS (Finance) degree from SP Jain. Shuttling between Mumbai and Bengaluru was part of his early working career. When I asked him how he landed up at Indya.com after working in the finance and treasury functions of large companies like Cipla, Microland and Alpic Finance, Lovaii replied, 'Everything just happened. It was 2000 and the dot-com mania was at its peak. I was almost forty and thought this was my last chance to get into a dot-com.' Lovaii joined media portal Indya.com, which was founded by his ex-boss and MMS batchmate, Microland founder and IT industry veteran, Pradeep Kar. In 2001, Kar sold (Ganapati, 2001) Indya.com to Rupert Murdoch-owned News Corp, which owned Star TV in India, in one of the most high-profile media-dot-com deals of that era. As Indya.com shut down, its executives turned to Lovaii for help in investing their settlement packages.

By November 2001, the post-9/11 market crash and the economic slowdown that would follow was engulfing the world and India. Despite the gloomy environment, Lovaii got an offer from ING Vysya, which he decided to turn down and opted for entrepreneurship instead. 'It was a bad time in the market, but I was enjoying advising people on their money, and that's what helped me in making up my mind,' he told me. Getting people to trust him with their money was not new to Lovaii since he was used to advising his colleagues on where to invest in his earlier jobs; his previous roles also helped Lovaii in meeting private sector mutual funds which were then new to India. 'When I was working at Alpic Finance, I met Templeton Mutual Fund (as it was known then) and they showed me the calculations for saving up and investing to pay for my child's education. Even today, I remember wishing someone had told me this ten years ago,' he said.

The idea of charging clients for investment advice and financial planning was a relatively new concept back in the early 2000s. But Lovaii had enough goodwill from his clients to start charging fees. The bull run in the Indian equity markets from 2003 to 2007 pushed the financial media to write extensively on personal finance. This tailwind helped many financial planners and advisers, including Lovaii. 'We used to publish financial plans in *Outlook Money* in the early/mid-2000s. We received many queries from readers on how much we charge for making these plans. However, when we sent our fee structure, there would be silence. All this changed during 2007/2008. The media's coverage on financial planning helped us,' he told me.

How does he deal with competition from wealth management desks at banks and specialized wealth management firms? 'That fear (of competition) was there initially. Clients need personalization and that is what we focus on. We customize for the client. We spend time on the person and not on the amount. I deal with the "I" (individual), not HNI (high-net-worth individual). I spend at least a couple of hours with people. I was lucky that people grew (in their financial goals and earnings) faster than me,' Lovaii told me. In 2016, TVS Capital took a majority stake in Lovaii's firm. When I asked him why he took this decision, he told me, 'I always wanted to make IMMPL an institution. I was on the lookout for tie-ups and a few people had shown interest. But eventually, someone from my advisory board connected me to Gopal Srinivasan (of TVS Capital) and once we got talking, I knew that they would not change my methods or my practice; most importantly, their values were aligned and that helped me make the decision.'

Lovaii's passion for financial planning is evident in his education and his affiliation with the industry. Lovaii was among the first professionals to get a CFP degree in India in 2004 and the first in India to get the CeFT certification in 2016. He is the founder–chairman (ex) of the Association of Registered Investment Advisers (ARIA, India) and has travelled extensively in the US/Europe for industry conferences on financial planning and related topics. Back in the early 2010s, at one of these conferences organized by the Financial Planning

Association (FPA, USA), he heard Susan Bradley, founder of the Sudden Money Institute (USA), talk about financial transitions. A few months prior to this, Lovaii was helping a widow of his friend, a businessman who had unexpectedly passed away. Not only did she have to deal with the traumatic event but also take over the reins of the business. 'At the FPA conference, I realized that this (financial transition) was exactly what I was dealing with. It was new to me but for the financial planners there, it was a topic that they were researching for the past decade. I enrolled in the course and told them that they must bring the course to India,' Lovaii told me.

When he signed up, Lovaii was initially worried that financial transition was too US-specific a topic to be brought to India, where the culture around death and financial transition was very different. 'Over time, I have learnt that human beings are pretty much the same all over the world. And by then, I had gone past the thrill of planning retirement for clients. I started getting interested in the behavioural aspect of personal finance. I knew that India was also a transition economy and as people got richer and the economy opened up to the world, there would be a need for knowledge on managing transitions.'

Building Blocks of Financial Planning

Lovaii believes that the basic building blocks of financial planning involve connecting a person's finances with his goals. He explained, 'There are five pieces—first, what am I earning? Second, what am I spending? Third, what are my assets? Fourth, what are my liabilities and commitments? And fifth—and the most crucial—what are my financial goals? With this data in place, you assume an expected rate of inflation and rate of return on debt and equity. Then, using a simple debt/equity allocation, we arrive at what you need to earn above that rate of inflation to meet your goals. We use that as a starting point. If the allocation matches with the goals, then that is great. If it does not, then it is time to ask the client what he is willing to sacrifice—his sleep or his goals,' he told me.

Once the basic work is done, the more comprehensive work of asset allocation, cashflows, emergency corpus, physical versus financial assets, etc., is set in motion. What are the major transition points that require us to be more careful with our finances? 'Two major transitions in life are death and divorce. Add to this, the sale of a business, inheritance, change in career, change in city and becoming empty nesters. At all these sensitive junctures in life, rationality goes out of the window since we are dealing with change,' he told me.

HNIs vs the Middle Class

Are HNIs different from the middle class? This was a topic about which Lovaii felt strongly and told me, 'HNI's don't know that they don't know whereas the middle class know they don't know, and they want help. Once you have more than what you need, you become lazy or you become experimental. I do not understand that—why would you want to lose money on an experiment? Many HNIs will say I do not want to put money in an equity mutual fund, but I will invest it in some unheard-of scheme because that will make for a good cocktail conversation. I think a lot of investment decisions for HNIs are done for cocktail conversations.' Finally, we wrap up with the common questions.

1. Where can I start learning about personal finance?

I wish we were taught about it in school. One of the things I learnt at the CeFT programme was that learning styles are different for different people. So, I think people should keep experimenting and learning. So whichever way they learn (audio, visual, reading books, watching videos, etc.) they should cross-verify that with one more source and then go forward— that is the way to start learning, in my opinion.

2. What are the basic minimum financial products that I should own?

Life insurance, health insurance, mutual funds and provident fund (PF, PPF) accounts.

3. Which do you prefer, stocks or mutual funds?

If you have the knowledge and can stomach the losses, and you can remove emotions from your investing decisions, you can look at stocks. But I look at mutual funds more like a building block and a must-have foundation. Once your investible surplus starts going higher, then maybe you can look at stocks because stocks give you a kick. But sometimes, stocks also give you a kick on the backside. So, we should be careful with stocks.

4. Active or passive mutual funds?

We prefer a combination because we do not think this is a mutually exclusive, either/or decision. After the recategorization of mutual funds, we prefer passive for the large cap (domestic and international investing) component of equities, whereas other parts of the portfolio can be active investment.

5. Should I buy or rent a house?

There is no single answer, and it varies from one person to another. One obvious reason to buy a house is that it makes you feel good, but you need to be careful with the overall allocation to that asset (house) and your cashflows. So, if a client already owns several houses, I would recommend not buying. But if it is a first-time buyer, first we'd check the allocation to that house and then see the size of the loan and whether the client can afford it; if he can't, we recommend alternatives like postponing the purchase, changing to a cheaper home (and/or location), etc. We need to remove our adviser bias here, where we go with blanket statements like 'mutual funds are best' or 'stocks are the way to go'. There is a place for everything.

6. What are your thoughts on FDs and debt funds?

Choose debt funds very carefully and patiently and through a lot of research, input and advice, and after you are sure you are willing to sit through the time horizon of the debt fund, because it is tougher to pick and choose debt than equity. For FDs, we do highlight the post-tax, post-inflation returns on FDs to our clients but there's also peace of mind in an FD.

7. Finally, what are your views on hot new investment areas like international investing and cryptocurrency?

We look only at regulated products and as of now (October 2021), cryptocurrency is a grey area. If a client insists, we tell them to put only the money they can afford to lose. For more than ten years, we have been recommending a 10–15 per cent allocation within equity towards regulated international products.

8. What are the five questions I should consider while choosing a financial adviser?

a. Choose between an individual or an organization, based on your needs.

b. What are the types of clients that this adviser has and does that match with your profile? If not, then get a reference for an adviser with clients of your profile.

c. Is your adviser licensed (RIA) or not? Obviously I am biased toward SEBI RIAs.

d. What is the fee structure, how does the RIA get compensated and what is the transparency of the fees in terms of what is hidden and what is not hidden?

e. Ask the adviser how he/she stays up to date? Take me for an example, I cannot boast that I did my CFP in the first batch of 2004 because it is all outdated and things change by the minute now.

4

The FIRE Dream

As seen in the previous chapter, technology has helped propel more people into investing than ever before in India. This has come at a time when India is slowly recovering from the pandemic and is poised for strong economic growth. Experts predict that the stock markets will follow suit in buoyancy. This chapter explains the opportunity and how you can use it to achieve your financial goals.

A Gigantic Opportunity Called India

It's hard not to be bullish on India. This is the view from the stock markets. Admittedly, this is a tainted view since the benchmark Sensex is up 203 per cent[1] in just over two years from the March 2020 pandemic's panic-driven lows. This scorching rally from the depths of despair was on pause at the time of writing but, as per experts, the best is yet to come. In May 2021, the business TV channel CNBC-TV18 quoted Motilal Oswal Financial Services chairman Raamdeo Agrawal's aggressive Sensex target of 2,00,000 in the next ten years:

Sensex can hit the 2-lakh mark in the next ten years, said veteran market expert Raamdeo Agarwal, indicating an annualised growth rate of nearly 15 per cent for the BSE frontline index from the current levels. Agrawal, chairman of Motilal Oswal Financial Services, also expects India to be a $5-trillion economy by FY29.

A few months later, in September 2021, the portal Moneycontrol. com carried (Moneycontrol Markets, 2021) an interview with Amar Ambani of YES Securities who gave a Sensex target of 1,25,000 by 2025:

What I can tell you with conviction is that the outlook for the next four years is extremely positive. In fact, I envision the Sensex hitting 125,000 by December of 2025, given the slew of conducive factors, including a pronounced business shift from the unorganised sector to the organised space, marked acceleration in the digital super cycle, sustained margins from the pandemic-enforced prudent cost management, all benefiting the listed space.

The bullishness of the market experts is being tested in 2022 as factors such as the Russia–Ukraine war, rising inflation driven by high commodity prices have driven sharp corrections in global stock markets, including India. Stock markets are unpredictable, and experts can go wrong.

Notwithstanding that, India's post-COVID-19 economic growth story is compelling. While India's GDP grew (MOSPI, Press Release, 2022) at a robust 8 per cent in FY16 and FY17, growth slowed to a 6 per cent CAGR in the next three years (FY18–FY20) and fell 8 per cent in the COVID-19-ravaged year of FY21. From this sharp fall, India's Ministry of Statistics and Programme Implementation (MOSPI) expects (Business

Standard Economy & Policy, 2022) a sharp rebound in FY22 with an advance estimate of 9.2 per cent in GDP growth. While this growth is off a low base, there are structural reasons for India's economic recovery. These are summarized in the table below taken from Slide 41 of HDFC Mutual Fund's Yearbook 2022.[2]

Indian Economy Outlook: Firing on Multiple Cylinders

Macroeconomic Environment	• Robust growth with broad-based improvement in consumption and investments • Comfortable external sector with large forex reserves, capital flows and favourable external environment • Gradual fiscal consolidation and range-bound inflation
Reforms	• In the period of COVID-19, the government has carried out several important reforms like Atmanirbhar Bharat programme, National Monetization Pipeline (NMP), creation of a 'bad bank', sector-specific measures, etc., creating a favourable environment for business and growth
Manufacturing, External Sector and China Plus One	• Rise in competitiveness of India's manufacturing as wages in China are ~2x of India's • Disruption led by COVID-19 likely to accelerate the shift of global supply chain to other EMs including India • PLI and measures like tax incentives, increase in import duties, etc.

Start-ups	• Start-up ecosystem set to expand driven by availability of risk capital, technical skills and supportive policies • Start-ups can help in employment generation, improving efficiency, creating wealth and driving innovation
Infrastructure, Capex and Housing	• Government's focus to boost infrastructure spend with NMP, National Infrastructure Pipeline (NIP), etc. • Private capex likely to pick up in medium term driven by robust demand, deleveraging and strong profitability • Real estate likely to revive driven by high affordability
Consumption	• Meaningful improvement in employment and new hiring, especially in organized segment • Digitization and improving e-commerce acceptability has given access to a larger customer base • Near-normal monsoon, higher crop sowing, pent up demand, wage inflation and higher savings

Source: HDFC Mutual Fund Yearbook 2022

In its World Economic Outlook released in October 2021, the International Monetary Fund stated that[3] India will retain its tag as the world's fastest growing economy. The confidence in India's prospects was best exemplified in the confident and optimistic speech given by Prime Minister Narendra Modi at the State of the World Address (Modi, 2022) at the World Economic Forum's Davos Summit in mid-January 2022. This extract is from his speech, and the emphasis in the text is mine:

India is committed to becoming a trusted partner in the world in global supply-chains. We are making way for free-trade agreement with many countries. The ability of Indians to adopt innovation, new technology; the spirit of entrepreneurship of Indians; can give new energy to every global partner of ours. *So, this is the best time to invest in India.*

Entrepreneurship among Indian youth is at a new height today. In 2014, where there were a few hundred registered start-ups in India, their numbers have crossed 60,000 today. It also has more than 80 unicorns, of which more than forty were formed in 2021 itself. Just as expat Indians are showing their skills on the global stage, in the same way Indian youth are fully ready, geared up to give new heights to all [sic] your businesses in India.

While it's easy to get carried away with this bullishness, there are two reasons to temper our expectations as well. Firstly, the pandemic is not over. At the time of writing this manuscript, the third wave of COVID-19, marked by the Omicron variant, has hit India. Unlike the previous two deadly waves, however, this wave has been more manageable so far and the medical infrastructure in large metro cities like Delhi and Mumbai is not getting overwhelmed. More importantly, India has made significant progress (Dey, 2022) with vaccination, covering 70 per cent of the adult population in the first year. I'm not a medical expert to make any assertions of how the COVID-19 virus will play out in the next few years. However, globally, in the past two years, the world is learning to tackle the virus—from vaccines to containment and coping strategies. I hope that these measures get even better as time goes by. Hence, the statements made in this chapter are under the generous assumptions that India's ability to handle the waves of the virus will continue to improve in the future.

Secondly, India's high rates of GDP growth are off a low base. And while India might be the fastest growing country in the world, we are not even in the top 100[4] when it comes to per capita income. Indeed, MOSPI data for the past three years (FY19 to FY22) shows that while India's per capita income in FY22 (Rs 1,07,801) has risen 8 per cent over FY21, it is still lower than the per capita income in FY19 (Rs 1,08,645). Put differently, the average Indian is still worse off in FY22 than he was in FY19. I can only hope that the growth story mentioned earlier plays out in full force and benefits the poorest sections of Indian society that were severely impacted by the pandemic.

Where to Start? From the Basics

A buoyant economy can help you in your career and business, and a sustained upturn in the stock markets can help you achieve your financial goals. And today, there are more people invested in the stock markets than ever before, as the table below shows:

Financial year (FY)	Total number of Demat accounts (in lakh at end-FY)	Increase in number of Demat accounts compared to previous year (in lakh)
2018–19	359	39
2019–20	409	50
2020–21	551	142
2021–22 (up to 31 October 2021)	738	187

Source: Ministry of Finance, Press Information Bureau (Ministry of Finance, 2021)

The surge in Demat accounts has been accompanied by a rise in stock market indices as well, with the Sensex also up to 52,974 as of 16 May 2022 from 33,255 as of 1 April 2018. There is a similar story playing out in mutual funds where the Systematic Investment Plan (SIP) has exploded in popularity. The share of SIP-related assets under management (AUMs) accounted for 15 per cent of total AUMs of the mutual fund industry in December 2021 and SIP AUMs have grown at a robust 35 per cent CAGR over the past five years (Shyam, ET Mutual Funds, 2022). While the average ticket size has fallen to Rs 2303 per account from Rs 3200 back in 2017 (Sanket Dhanorikar, 2017), the number of accounts has increased significantly, resulting in monthly SIP flows now becoming an important source of liquidity for stock markets. More importantly, the money invested in mutual funds is becoming more patient. More than half of retail equity mutual funds holdings as of September 2021 had stayed in the market for more than two years (Kiran, 2022). Rising stock markets have been a key driver in retail participation, but the bigger story is the rise of awareness of investing and good financial habits among the broader population. Given India's population, this is just the beginning.

So, where do you start? I spoke with veteran personal finance journalist and head of personal finance at Moneycontrol.com, Kayezad E. Adajania, and asked him where and how does a twenty-five-year-old, who has just got his/her first job, start on his investment journey. 'He or she can choose from a) online portals and investment apps, and b) mutual fund distributors (MFDs). At that age they wouldn't have money (or a large enough corpus) to pay the fees for a financial adviser, so it makes sense to check out the various portals and smartphone apps that offer investment services for free. MFDs also do this for you and help you get started. Keep in mind that since these services are offered for free, the mutual fund schemes that are offered might be regular schemes which are more expensive than direct schemes,' he told me. However, he added a note of caution that one needs to be careful with online/app-based advice since these services might show you the best performing mutual fund schemes and not the one ideally suited for your risk return profile. Over time, and when one can afford the services, Kayezad believes that holistic, goal-based financial planning from a SEBI RIA should be considered.

Another approach to investing, that Kayezad recommends, is a goal-based approach. A common mistake that many of us make while investing is to see all investments from the point of view of returns. We check past returns, tend to invest in recent good performers and measure our portfolio only in terms of returns. A better way is to fix your money goals and then work your way to meet them. This means, you decide how much money you need after 'x' number of years; this could be for your child's education, a foreign holiday, a new home and so on. Then, you work backwards and decide how much money you need to invest every month and then, simply monitor your progress. The good thing about this approach is that if you meet your goals, your returns would have been automatically taken care of. And financial goals are the reason why you invest and save, right? Your money must fulfil some purpose. If the purpose is fulfilled, your money has done its job', he told me.

Ashal Jauhari, moderator of the ASAN Ideas for Wealth Group, told me, 'Learning about personal finance is no rocket science. In all my interactions, I start with the basics, namely— do you have adequate term insurance? Do you have adequate health insurance? Do you have an adequate emergency corpus? And have you identified your goals?' he told me. 'Most of the time, people first pick the investment products and invest, and then try to link their lives and their goals with these products. Essentially, it's the other way around. First, we should understand our needs, our requirements and then match the products to them. If you ask me, my standard answer for personal finance is to use common sense, although people don't use common sense in most investment decisions; that's another problem in itself.'

Professor Pattabiraman of the *Freefincal* blog told me that an appreciation of basic common sense is the only prerequisite necessary to learn about managing money. 'Two questions— what exactly is my need, and how do I create a solution for this need?—encompass all of personal finance. The number one mistake in personal finance is placing products, returns and saving tax above individual needs,' he told me. He had an even simpler answer to the question of where one starts to learn about personal finance. 'Enquire within upon everything.[5] Almost all money management answers lie within us. The more time we spend introspecting about what we truly want, the more precise our choices become,' he told me. You can find more tips on where to start learning about personal finance in the RIA interviews that accompany each chapter in this book.

The FIRE Dream

The FIRE that Ashal refers to above is short for financially independent, retiring early. In the USA, the Wikipedia page[6] on 'The FIRE Movement' calls it a model that became 'particularly popular among millennials in the 2010s'. The movement is so popular that the *Wall Street Journal* (Lam, 2019) termed the 2010s as '. . . the decade when being thrifty became socially acceptable'. A 2018 article (Tergesen & Dagher, 2018) on FIRE titled 'The New Retirement Plan: Save Almost Everything, Spend Virtually Nothing', again in the *WSJ*, generated more than 1000 comments. Social media is full of FIRE content across popular platforms such as

Instagram, Twitter and YouTube. The FIRE subreddit[7] has more than one million members with even deeper subreddits such as r/leanfire, r/fatFIRE and r/frugal. The central tenet of FIRE is frugality and cutting back on expenditure today to save aggressively for the future with the goal of retiring early, ideally at forty years, much ahead of the more widely accepted norm of sixty-five years.

FIRE is new and exciting to America, given their culture of consumerism and the millennial tag line #YOLO (you only live once). And what's exciting in the USA ends up being wildly popular in India as well. Indians know frugality only too well; for example, abstinence from excesses and frugality is advocated in many religions such as Buddhism and Jainism. Religions apart, we are too familiar with cutting costs, getting the best deal and indulging in what's popularly called 'jugaad'. 'India is to frugality as Bethlehem is to Jesus,' wrote (Giridharadas, 2008) the *New York Times* columnist Anand Giridharadas in 2008.

In July 2019, I was lucky to sit in a meeting with Professor Sanjay Bakshi, managing partner at ValueQuest Capital LLP and Saurabh Mukherjea for our book *The Victory Project*. Sanjay, who was also then the adjunct professor at Management Development Institute, Gurugram, is hugely popular in social media for his writings on finance and investing which can be accessed on his *Fundoo Professor* blog and his Twitter account. When Saurabh asked Sanjay, 'What does a young student of Prof. Bakshi who wants to succeed in life learn from our conversation?', Sanjay replied 'Financial independence and the thrill of frugality.' Sanjay told his students to focus intensely on becoming financially independent by spending only what's left after investing a majority of their disposable income. 'This should be the method for many, many years and that is how one gets to be financially independent,' he told us. You can read the full conversation at the end of Chapter 3 of our book (Mukherjea & Gupta, *The Victory Project: Six Steps to Peak Potential*, 2020).

This is indeed a great time to start your journey in personal finance. The optimism around India's economic prospects, the move towards financial savings from physical savings (discussed in the opening chapters), and the FIRE dream have all driven the creation of an industry of financial content aimed at people hungry to learn more. Books, such as these, are being written, podcasts (such as *Paisa Vaisa*, hosted by me on IVM Podcasts) are being recorded, hundreds of thousands of videos on YouTube are being uploaded, tweet upon tweet upon tweet are being typed on Twitter, and Instagram stories and photos are going out every day to satiate the hunger of learning. The good news? You are spoilt for choice to learn about personal finance. The bad news? You might land up taking the wrong advice and burning your fingers.

A booming stock market, wildly gyrating cryptocurrencies and a large enough number of people hungry to make a quick buck will also give rise to shady schemes and scams. Here are a few examples from the recent past:

- In January 2022, the capital markets watchdog SEBI cracked down on a stock recommendation scam that used Twitter and Telegram. As per this article (Gawande, 2022) in *Mint*, 'According to the Sebi order, these individuals were giving unsolicited stock recommendations using social media channels to manipulate stock prices and make illegal profits.'
- As per another *Mint* article,[8] 'Indians visited crypto scam websites more than 17.8 million times in 2020. The figure fell sharply in 2021, but it was still substantial at 9.6 million times.'

• Stockbrokers cheating investors isn't new, and stock market volatility during the pandemic in 2020 unearthed questionable doings at Anugrah Stock & Broking. In August 2020, Moneylife reported (Dalal, Moneylife, 2020) on potential trouble at the brokerage and eventually in March 2021, SEBI imposed (*Economic Times*, 2021) a fine on the firm after finding that it had misused client funds.

So, how does one get started on chasing and achieving their financial dreams? The final two chapters will answer this question comprehensively for readers.

Adviser Perspectives: Melvin Joseph

SEBI registration number: INA000015534
Website: www.finvin.in

Melvin Joseph runs Finvin Financial Planners (FFP) along with his wife, Tesy Paul. Melvin has a CFP degree from FPSB, a PG diploma in financial advising from Indian Institute of Banking and Finance, and a PG diploma in public relations and advertising from Public Relations Society of India. Melvin started his financial planning practice as a proprietorship firm in 2010 and got his SEBI RIA license in 2013 as an individual which he then converted to a partnership in 2020. Melvin's fees are not linked to assets under advisement, which is the predominant model for most fee-based SEBI RIAs. Melvin charges fees based on three categories of clients, namely, i) resident Indians, ii) non-resident Indians (NRIs), and iii) senior citizens and single mothers with liquid assets up to Rs 1 crore. I spoke with Melvin on 4 October 2021.

Melvin has two decades of work experience with some of India's largest insurance firms. His last job was in 2010 as country head, Institutional Alliances, SBI Life. FFP has more than 400 public reviews on Google Reviews with a stellar rating of 4.8 out of 5; you can check them out by typing 'Finvin Financial Planners' on Google Maps. Professor Pattabiraman of the popular *Freefincal* blog told me that 'Melvin is a man of extraordinary dedication, integrity, courage, compassion and enterprise'.

Melvin hails from Idukki district, which is known as the spice capital of Kerala. He got his bachelor's degree in physics from Newman College in Thodupuzha and—like many younger, lower middle-class Indians—his biggest aim after college was to get a job to support his father. LIC gave him this job and for the next eleven years (1989 to 2000), Melvin worked in various roles across LIC's branches in Kerala and Tamil Nadu. Melvin is also academically strong, which helped him pass exams from the Insurance Institute of India and move up within LIC.

In the mid-to-late 1990s, India's insurance sector opened up to private sector companies and in 2000, Melvin came to Mumbai to join Reliance Industries ahead of their planned foray into insurance. However, this venture didn't progress as Melvin expected, and he then joined Kotak Life Insurance in 2001. From 2003 to 2005, Melvin worked for Bajaj Allianz Life Insurance and in 2005, Melvin joined SBI Life. In 2010, Melvin left SBI Life to start his financial planning practice.

Melvin had a very successful corporate career but eventually, the changing nature of the insurance industry in the late 2000s convinced Melvin to strike out on his own. 'By God's grace, my team's performance was on top in all companies which helped me in fast-track promotion and lots of rewards including overseas trips. I visited more than ten countries during this period. I was selling all types of policies through my team. Till 2003, it was only traditional policies after which unit-linked insurance plans (ULIPs) became popular. Some of the ULIPs had exorbitant charges and it was not good for the investors. Insurance companies came out with more innovative policies. Most of them were not good for policyholders. Slowly, it started pricking my conscience and I decided to leave this sector in 2010,' he told me.

Melvin's humble roots in Kerala and his parents' struggle
left a deep imprint on his mind. 'My father did not have a
steady income during my childhood, and my mother decided to
be a housewife to take care of me and my siblings. I have seen
the practical difficulties of not having a regular income and lack
of financial planning. I believe that money is not everything in
life, but without money, we are nothing,' he told me.

Melvin's experience in the life insurance industry pushed
him to look out for the common man. 'I interacted with all types
of people in my corporate life, but I really enjoyed interacting
with middle class people the most. I get immense satisfaction
in creating star performers from ordinary people. I strongly
believe that the middle class need this (financial planning)
service, but they don't realize it,' he told me. But getting the
middle class to pay for financial planning was not easy at all and
the early years were tough. 'I started my practice with the motto
of offering unbiased advice at affordable prices. This resulted in
little income in the initial years of my practice. I lived on my
savings from 2010 to 2015. Many well-wishers asked me to
go back to a corporate job. But I was confident of my success
because I believe this is a service which everyone needs,' he said.

Eventually, Melvin's patience paid off, and today, he enjoys
a lot of goodwill among his clients. As is evident from his
reviews, his clients are happy. 'Now, I am getting more clients
than I can manage. I am enjoying this because my clients are
happy, and they are investing in good products which are good
for their family,' he told me.

What Is Financial Planning?

Financial planning, however, remains a new concept. Many
clients come to Melvin with misplaced assumptions such
as a) financial planning is some kind of magic that creates

extraordinary returns, and b) financial planning means managing investments. This is why at the very beginning of his engagement Melvin informs his clients that financial planning is not about maximizing returns but about planning for financial goals through instruments that are commensurate with their risk-taking ability.

Melvin firmly believes that financial planning should be the top priority for middle-class salaried employees. 'The middle-class man has to plan for his vital financial goals with limited resources. He cannot afford to make mistakes with his limited income. Children's higher education and marriage, retirement planning, buying a house, a car and going on a vacation are some of his priorities. He should also plan for term insurance, health insurance, etc.,' he told me.

Approach to Financial Planning

Melvin's approach to financial planning begins with two basic building blocks—a backup plan to deal with any exigency, and investment planning through a mix of equity and debt instruments. Within equity, Melvin advises a mix of index funds, flexi-cap funds, and mid-cap funds. Within debt, Melvin prefers government savings scheme such as provident fund (in all forms namely employee, voluntary and public) and Sukanya Samriddhi Yojana (for clients with daughters). He also advises debt mutual funds to his clients.

I asked Melvin's advice for a twenty-five-year-old starting his career with the aim of a) retiring at age sixty-five, and b) quit his job at age forty to launch his own start-up. Melvin said, 'In the first case, retirement is forty years away. If he is disciplined and starts investing in the right products from twenty-five, he can achieve financial freedom in twenty years. He can have high allocation to equity for the first 10–15 years and then gradually rebalance the portfolio. But if he is planning to quit his job at forty, he must plan it differently. He should first plan to create the necessary amount of money required for the start-up. At some point of time, he should start thinking about creating enough money to manage monthly expenses a few years from when he turns forty and until he is back on a good income. Along with these, he should plan for his retirement through a mix of equity and debt products.' Wrapping up the questionnaire, these were Melvin's answers to some commonly asked questions in personal finance.

1. Where should I start to learn about managing my money?

Personal finance is a simple topic and very important for every individual. Unfortunately, financial literacy is very bad in our country. Good and conflict-free books are rare in personal finance. You can read the book *Let's Talk Money* by Monika Halan. You can join the Facebook group Asan Ideas for Wealth. You can read blogs like *Freefincal*, *Subramoney*, etc. Though personal finance is a boring subject, you should develop a taste for it.

2. What are the basic minimum financial products that I should own?

Public provident fund (PPF) is an evergreen option within debt category. Equity mutual funds can create wealth in the long term. Systematic Investment Plan (SIP) in equity funds will help you in wealth creation through disciplined investing. Term insurance for the breadwinner and health insurance for the family are also essential.

3. Should I choose stocks, or should I choose mutual funds? Within stocks, how do I build frameworks or models to choose stocks?

Stock picking is a specialized job, which requires lots of efforts and skill. It is not everyone's cup of tea. In equity mutual funds, the fund manager does this job with a team of experts to support him. For a retail investor, equity mutual fund is better than stocks because of this professional stock selection. If you invest in direct plans of mutual funds, the annual fund management charge is around 1 per cent. If a highly educated person with more than fifteen years of fund management experience is available to manage my investment at a cost of 1 per cent per year, I feel, it is worth paying for it.

4. Within mutual funds, how do I decide between active and passive?

I suggest a mix of active and passive funds to clients. Within large-cap funds, the scope for generating higher returns is limited because of the recent SEBI regulations. So, I suggest passive index funds within large-cap category. Other than this, I suggest active funds within flexi-cap and mid-cap categories.

5. Should I buy a house or rent a house?

You can have one house for self-use. But I don't suggest real estate as investment because rental yield is one of the lowest in India and the scope for appreciation is also limited. The golden days of real estate are almost over. Till you are sure about where you want to settle down, renting is better.

6. On the fixed income side, are FDs of any use? How should I choose debt funds?

FDs are the darling investment option for most of us. But after factoring the tax on interest, the net return from FD is too little.

You can consider debt funds in lieu of FDs as part of the debt portfolio. Debt funds are tax efficient compared to FDs because of the indexation benefits for holding of more than three years. Within debt funds, there are many categories. I suggest only liquid funds and ultra-short-term debt funds to clients. They carry little interest rate risk and credit risk. You can consider gilt funds if you are comfortable with the volatility depending on the intertest rate movement.

7. What about new investment areas like international investing and cryptocurrency?

You can have a portion of your equity portfolio in international mutual fund schemes. You have many options now to invest in overseas funds through index funds. But long-term outlook from Indian funds is better because India is a developing country. I avoid cryptocurrency because of the high volatility in it and the legality issues. I don't exactly know how it works!

8. What are the five questions that I should always ask myself before making an investment/purchase/financial decision?

a. Is this investment going to help me reach my financial goals?
b. Is the investment product equity or debt?
c. Does this investment product have a regulator like RBI or SEBI?
d. Is this investment one-time, or will there be a commitment for many years?
e. Is there an option for premature exit/sale?
f. And finally, how do I redeem this investment on maturity?

5

A Framework for the Future

How do you realize your financial dreams and prosper in your financial journey? The final two chapters of this book will answer these questions. This chapter points you in the right direction and the final chapter provides you with a few maps. The first step is an absolute basic one and a good place to start— how to learn about personal finance. All of us must have basic minimum knowledge about financial products and how they are useful in our lives. Over time, and once we need one, we can always consult a financial adviser. This chapter will deal with both aspects—self-learning and how financial advisers operate.

How to Begin

In the past few years, I've often heard complaints on the lines of 'I wish schools and colleges taught us more about money'. Without going into the merits of the complaint or commenting on our education system, I make one confident assertion— there is enough out there for you to start learning irrespective of your age. This book is a humble attempt. If we didn't learn about handling our finances in school, that doesn't mean we stay ignorant all our lives. The Internet opened access to tomes of literature on personal finance across visual formats like books and videos and audio formats like podcasts. You only need to ask yourself two questions: How much time in a day can you dedicate to learning, and what is your preferred way of learning, i.e., do you prefer written, video or audio content? In my experience, you will eventually adapt yourself to all three in varying amounts. There are only twenty-four hours in a day, and you have a day job. So set up a schedule that is convenient to you and begin your journey.

While there are various ways to learn, I prefer setting up a strong foundation and then updating your knowledge. Books set up this foundation and the Internet can help you update your knowledge. Often, the authors (or their firms) of the books recommended below have a significant presence on social media and following them should keep you on track. However, before you track them on social media, please track the time you spend on social media. There are hundreds, possibly thousands, of online groups and influencers across social media and getting caught up in daily content can be an enormous waste of your time. Be judicious and disciplined with your time. Your long-term goals do not depend on the daily gyrations of the stock market or the latest stock tip or idea from your WhatsApp groups. Be very careful in how you tread the murky waters of social media. Choose your content carefully and be judicious with your time.

With that important warning, here's a list of my top five authors that can help you get started. My purpose is to get you to understand basic aspects of investments (such as risk, return, liquidity, taxation, etc.), how financial products like stocks, insurance, mutual funds and credit cards work, and most importantly, make you aware of your relationship with money. These books, in my view, are the building blocks to setting up your finances for life. Four of these five authors have been on my podcast, and it was an honour to host them.

1. Saurabh Mukherjea: Obviously I'm biased since Saurabh has written the introduction to this book, and my working relationship with Saurabh goes back a few years. I had the honour of being the co-author on *The Victory Project* and having worked with him as a consultant from 2014 to 2018. If you can forgive the bias, then I recommend all of Saurabh's books, namely, *Gurus of Chaos* (Mukherjea, *Gurus of Chaos: Modern India's Money Masters*, 2015), *The Unusual Billionaires* (Mukherjea, *The Unusual Billionaires*, 2016), *Coffee Can Investing* (Mukherjea, Ranjan & Uniyal, *Coffee Can Investing: The Low-Risk Road to Stupendous Wealth*, 2018), *The Victory Project* (Mukherjea & Gupta, *The Victory Project: Six Steps to Peak Potential*, 2020) and *Diamonds in the Dust* (Mukherjea, Ranjan & Desai, *Diamonds in the Dust: Consistent Compounding for Extraordinary Wealth Creation*, 2021). If I had to choose just one of these, I'd go for *Coffee Can Investing* but I thoroughly recommend that you read the others too. You can also follow Saurabh and his team's thinking at the Marcellus newsletters which are free for subscription on their website: www.marcellus.in.

2. Monika Halan: Disclosure yet again. Monika helped me extensively for this book. Biases apart, I think Monika is the gold standard in personal finance writing in India. She is unbiased, sharp and insightful when it comes to handling your money. In a world of influencers peddling paid content, Monika calls it straight and has often taken the industry to task for shady practices. Being a veteran adds heft and credibility. Her book, *Let's Talk Money* (Halan, 2018) is a must-read if you wish to learn how financial products work in India and how they are relevant to your needs. Monika is

also present across social media and blogs at monikahalan. wordpress.com.

3. Deepak Shenoy: Deepak heads CapitalMind and his first book, *Moneywise* (Shenoy, 2021), was launched late last year. The book is easy to understand and full of anecdotes, including some from Deepak's life, that are useful for the reader to relate to in his own life. I have known Deepak since he started CapitalMind and his success speaks volumes about his abilities. Deepak is also present on social media and CapitalMind has a subscription product to which I am subscribed to.

4. Morgan Housel: Morgan Housel's *The Psychology of Money* (Housel, 2020) has sold millions of copies across the world. Morgan brings a refreshing change in personal finance literature because he combines learnings across multiple diverse fields from history to psychology into managing your money. Morgan is present on social media and writes regularly at the Collaborative Fund's blog: https://www. collaborativefund.com/blog/.

5. Ben Carlson: Ben Carlson's *A Wealth of Common Sense* (Carlson, 2015) is a great book to understand how to use two critical things—simplicity and common sense—in your financial plans. So many of us are put off by financial decisions because finance is full of jargon and complexity. In his book, Carlson explains how that's not the case and how we can keep things simple and yet achieve our financial goals. Ben is active on social media and runs a website: https://www.awealthofcommonsense.com.

Why are there only five books and not ten? To keep things simple and help you start off. In these dopamine-fuelled, social media-addicted (Goldman, *Scope Blog*) world, reading a book is considered a major challenge. People now prefer bite-sized knowledge in the form of three-minute videos, 140-character tweets, stories on Instagram and five-line messages on WhatsApp. I think if you can finish even half of the books mentioned above, you would have started well on your journey. If you're still hungry to read more, then you will get many recommendations from the books themselves and from the updates of the authors mentioned above. Saurabh, for example, is a voracious reader and if you're subscribed to his newsletter, you'll have enough reading material to keep you busy.

As you progress in your financial journey, you might run out of time to manage your money. Many of us have day jobs, and as we grow old, our responsibilities increase and at some point, we might need a financial adviser. The next section helps you navigate the world of financial advice.

The World of Financial Advisers

Trust is the crux of all advice. And lack of trust is among the most commonly cited response to the question, 'What stops you from hiring a financial adviser?' The surge in interest in personal finance and the influx of many—often young—people into the world of investments have driven a hunger for learning about money. An industry of experts has sprung up in response, ranging from young social media influencers to veterans of stock markets. Where previously we'd ask our elders, or professionals like our chartered accountant or friendly neighbourhood mutual fund distributor, for the best investment advice, today we simply tune into our favourite YouTube channel or Instagram account or—indeed—our favourite podcast. Today, there's tonnes of advice, almost all of it available for free. Not all of this advice is good, or even well suited for you. As with most things in life, everything depends on your personal needs and specific requirements.

Financial products have always been 'pushed' to you. Your bank is typically the first financial product that you own and the centre of all your financial transactions. Ideally, your bank should suggest financial products based on your financial history and your requirements. Instead, banks tend to sell products that are profitable for them. A simple online search for the phrase 'mis-selling by banks' will give you enough articles that have been written on this topic. A *Business Standard* article from February 2021 states that banks and brokers receive (Panda, 2021) the highest number of mis-selling complaints than any distribution channel.

Network FP is India's leading online knowledge platform for financial advisers. I spoke at length with Sadique Neelgund, director at Network FP. In 2004, Sadique worked in the wealth division of a large bank and recognized the problem, namely the sales-driven, product-centric approach followed by the bank instead of what was required—a solution-oriented, client-centric approach. That's why he and his wife, Priti, started Network FP to support the financial advisory profession in India and help it grow. The journey, however, has only begun because trust remains an issue. 'Trust in a person or profession is a matter of confidence in (a) integrity/ethical conduct, and (b) competence/capability. The consumer is clueless about who is a good financial adviser, where can she find them, where can she verify their background, how to really work with the adviser for best results, how they are compensated, etc. Consumers have burned their fingers while working with financial intermediaries like sophisticated bankers and friendly agents. Consumers have also burned their fingers by doing it on their own thanks to messed up portfolios, costly products, wrong timings, etc.,' he told me.

At the heart of the problem is the fine line between investment advice and financial planning. Most people look for investment advice and not financial planning—which is like looking for weight loss and not fitness. Nothing wrong with that, but like weight loss is just one part of our overall fitness, investment advice is just one part of financial planning. Limiting financial planning to investment advice might put you off track because the world of financial products can be complicated and even the best advice is short-sighted if it doesn't consider things like your risk profile, your long-term goals, base rates, inflation, etc. For example, you started a ten-year SIP and patiently stayed the course only to find that the SIP couldn't even beat its benchmark, what do you do? Or, you bought a second home because your friend doubled his money in the previous five years but in the past decade, you've not even beaten inflation. At the other extreme are examples of people feeling dejected because their stock portfolio only doubled in value whereas their friends who invested in cryptocurrency (or the hottest start-up in town) are laughing all the way to the crypto exchange. Financial planning, thus, is more than just investment advice. However, the financial adviser industry is still a work in progress in the current set of regulations. Sadique outlined the following areas which are creating hurdles for the financial adviser community in India:

1) The SEBI RIA regulations' entry barrier and compliance is so high that the majority of the existing and aspiring financial advisers will stay out of it.

2) RIA regulations have mixed up stock research and tip providers with comprehensive financial planners, with a majority of RIAs comprising the former. Clearly, it's an identity or positioning problem.

3) Mutual fund distributors (MFDs) do much more than just recommending mutual funds; they do insurance, loans, P2P, PMS, etc. And RIAs do so much more than just

investment advisory; they do financial planning, insurance planning, taxation, etc. So, the nomenclature of MFD and RIA is narrow and does not accurately represent the actual work done.

4) Consumer awareness is happening at a product-level or service-level, whereas it should ideally happen holistically at the consumer-level from neutral educators or educational bodies.

This discussion brings us to the obvious question—how does one get good financial advice? There are two obvious answers—DIY (do it yourself) or hire a specialist. The DIY approach works well when we are young and can dedicate time and effort to learning about money and finance. A lot of people think that personal finance is full of difficult jargon that's not easy to understand, and this is mostly true. However, if you commit yourself to a learning plan and then follow the plan in a focused way, you stand a good chance of learning how to handle your money. This is similar to following a plan for your health (diet, exercise, etc.). The forums mentioned earlier—like ASAN Ideas for Wealth—are full of people who have no background in money and finance and are yet very well versed in financial products. So, arming yourself with basic knowledge and then keeping yourself updated (as mentioned earlier, by reading books and following the authors) should work for you to a reasonably large extent. And when it comes to choosing specific financial products, you can even get help online from sources that you identify and trust.

However, as we grow old and our responsibilities increase, the time that we can dedicate to learning and staying updated on personal finance, reduces. This is when you need a good adviser and in the next chapter, we make a list of questions that will help you find one. As mentioned earlier, the field of advisory is still new and growing. So, there are a range of advisers to choose from, starting with online financial planning services that provide robo-advisories for a fee, all the way to SEBI RIAs such as those interviewed in this book. What you finally decide will depend on a lot of factors, such as your ease with using technology, your preference for a human adviser, the level of service that you need, etc. The questions in the next chapter should help you get started.

Adviser Perspectives: Suresh Sadagopan

SEBI registration number: INA000016001
Website: https://ladder7.co.in/

Suresh Sadagopan is among the most respected financial planners in India. He formed Ladder7 Financial Advisories in 2004 and is at the forefront of the fast-growing financial planning industry. Suresh has an MMS degree from BITS Pilani and was among the first planners in India to get the CFP licence from FPSB India in 2005. He strengthened his financial planning credentials with the CTEP (chartered trust and estate planner) licence from the American Academy of Financial Management in 2016 and the registered life planner licence from the Kinder Institute (USA) in 2019.

Suresh is a firm believer in advocacy and leads various industry initiatives such as ARIA (as a board member), Financial Planners Guild of India (founder and current president), Network FP (past member on their advisory board) and FPSB India (past board member). Suresh is among the most visible faces in industry events as well as in the media. Suresh is also the author of the book *If God Was Your Financial Planner* (Sadagopan, 2020). We spoke on 13 October 2021, and what follows is an edited version of our conversation.

Suresh graduated from the reputed BITS Pilani in 1987 and began his career in the information technology (IT) industry, first as an employee for just over three years and then as an entrepreneur running an IT training and products firm with partners for six years. What pushed him towards financial products? 'By the early 2000s, the Internet was making a lot of businesses redundant. Many companies from whom we were sourcing products were either closing or moving to other product lines. Suddenly, our product pipeline was drying up and I had no choice but to look for alternative business options. Around that time (2002), the private sector in insurance was opening up in India, and it looked like a good opportunity. I was always in touch with the markets and economy, and financial services looked like a good place to switch to. Also, I wanted a business where I did not have to invest much and was instead looking to use my knowledge and skills. Financial services fit that bill and I made my entry through insurance,' Suresh told me.

Suresh began his financial career in life insurance products. Insurance companies give their distributors client profilers which helped them understand their clients' needs better and recommend an appropriate insurance policy. Suresh converted four of every ten prospects into clients which was much better than the then-prevailing average of one in ten. Suresh also liked the idea of sitting with clients and understanding their financial needs and aspirations. Financial planning then became a logical progression, and when the FPSB launched the CFP course in India, Suresh signed up and got his CFP license.

Over the years, Suresh picked up specialized training in estate planning and life planning. He is a big believer in the idea that financial planning is an important part of planning for life. 'Life planning is a way of understanding what gives us a deep sense of fulfilment, happiness, a sense of purpose and the zest to look forward to the future with excited anticipation.

Our motivations in life give us our goals and only after understanding goals can one create a financial plan. Doing life planning and financial planning together gives the best results for a person,' he told me.

Returns from Investment or Returns from Life

Suresh is a big believer in process and discipline, and his firm's name, Ladder 7, symbolizes progression toward success in life. He firmly believes that financial planning is not about investment returns but about returns from life. Thus, financial planning enables you to live a fulfilling life filled with happiness, contentment, achievement, authenticity and reaching one's potential. 'Our financial architecture makes (our client's) life meaningful instead of making them chase more money and run after investment returns while living a meaningless existence with stress and anxiety,' he told me.

Understanding Financial Goals

Suresh starts with understanding his client's goals and the time frames within which to achieve them, given their current financial situation. Suresh then provides various options on how to achieve these goals, and once the client has chosen his option, the financial plan is developed further into a blueprint. The client's existing assets and investments are analysed and aligned to the goals, including suggesting new investments and getting out of inappropriate ones. 'Getting the appropriate asset mix is important and the asset allocation we suggest is based on the client's risk profile, return requirements, liquidity and income needs, and tax implications,' he said. The planning exercise culminates in an action plan to be followed for the next twelve months and reviewed every six months. 'The process is aimed at keeping our client on the path of wealth creation and financial freedom for our clients,' he told me.

How does Suresh resolve the problem of client expectations (high returns) versus sticking to a goal-oriented process? 'This is a classic problem. Clients have this wrong notion that they will do well in life only if they get the highest returns on their portfolio. So, they keep chasing fads and churning needlessly—which is harmful since it can result in higher risks, penalties and higher taxes. Life's important goals are sacrosanct, and our financial plans are constructed to meet these goals, and not necessarily achieve the highest returns,' he emphasized.

Why Is Financial Planning Useful?

Financial planning is also useful in navigating unexpected and often unpleasant situations in our lives. Suresh gave me three examples:

1. A client met with an accident and needed long hospitalization and eventually had to leave his job. We worked to get the insurance payout and ensure that the client's family had sufficient income to take care of their expenses and goals.
2. A client was going through a harrowing time at work and wanted to resign at short notice. We worked towards a planned resignation to ensure that his financial needs were met post resignation. He resigned eventually and went to his hometown where he is leading a much happier and is well-provided-for.
3. A client was going through a separation with his wife and their son wanted to stay with his mother. Our client sought advice on the settlement process. We worked on the case and suggested a fair settlement to take care of his wife

and son. The case was settled amicably, and our client is assisting his son for his college education.

Planned Approach to Life and Money

In a preliminary conversation, Suresh told me that when choosing clients, he preferred to avoid high-net-worth individuals (known as HNIs), typically from business backgrounds. I found that interesting given that most RIAs would love to build a practice based on large AUMs. 'We're building a sustainable practice based on the philosophy of a planned approach to life and money. So, we want clients who are aligned to our vision and—most importantly—trust the adviser. In my experience, businesspeople do not believe much in planning and tend to take sudden, ad hoc decisions. Their success (in their business) makes them cocky about their investments. They take decisions on their own and dictate how investment decisions should be made. They expect high returns on the portfolios we suggest. They compare returns on their business with returns on our recommended portfolios without understanding that we (not them) are planning their personal finances and are de-risking by investing in avenues outside of their business,' he told me.

He added that HNIs divide their portfolios among many advisers without telling them, which leads to advisers making recommendations oblivious to the overall portfolio. 'This is not financial planning, these are just random investments,' he told me. Suresh prefers senior corporate executives and finds them more aligned to Ladder7's philosophy. He summarized his approach as follows, 'We are very selective in the kind of clients we onboard. We are not too bothered about turning down business and do not have any aggressive AUM targets since we are not in any competition. We are content in building a sustainable practice where we have excellent relationships with our clients who stay with us for life. There is hardly any firefighting in our business due to the way we onboard clients. That is the way we like it.'

What Should a Beginner Do?

As we begin on the commonly asked questions and I ask Suresh where a beginner can start learning about money and finance, Suresh says, 'It is all around us—books, magazines, newspapers, portals, blogs, podcasts and TV channels. Post COVID-19, there is a blizzard of webinars on personal finance. Knowledge and information are available aplenty, we just need to go out there and access it in a form that works for us and use it to our benefit,' he told me.

What Financial Products Should One Buy?

Suresh does not believe in a common set of must-have financial products for everyone since everyone's needs are specific. However, he believes that equity-oriented products (mutual funds, stocks, PMS, etc.) and debt products (FDs, mutual funds, PPF, savings schemes, etc.) should be part of portfolios in proportions dependent on one's life stage and goals. Gold and real estate can also be added depending on requirements. Within equities, Suresh prefers mutual funds. 'Mutual fund managers are well qualified, experienced and have access to professional resources and a team to support them in the research and investments.' On passive versus active investing in equities, Suresh admits that passive products are beating active products in both large-caps and mid-caps but suggests that the choice between active and passive should be based on a client's current situation and goals in the future.

Buy or Rent a House?

On buy versus rent, Suresh believes that renting is a practical solution early in life, whereas buying a home can be considered later when one has decided to stay in that home and not relocate to another city. 'At the earlier stages in one's life, it may be sensible to rent a home because a) one may not have the resources to buy a home, especially one large enough for the family, b) in the early stages of their career, people tend to be mobile and move from city to city or even to another country, and c) one may want to stay nearer the office (to avoid long commutes in cities) and such homes might not be affordable enough to buy early in one's career. For all those reasons, renting is a great option till later in life when one has decided to settle down,' he said.

FDs vs Debt Mutual Funds

On the debate between FDs and debt mutual funds, Suresh believes that FDs are low-yielding products that might work for those in the nil or lower tax regime if they want a product that is low on risk and offers regular returns. 'For those in a higher income bracket, FDs aren't suitable since they aren't tax-efficient and offer interest rates lower than inflation—so you will be eroding your wealth. Debt funds are a much better choice provided you do not need the income and can stay invested for three years and above (to qualify for long-term capital gains). For those who can stay invested in the long term, longer duration funds are appropriate and conversely, short duration funds are for short-term needs. Whatever your requirement is, it may be a better choice to invest in schemes that hold high quality credit papers,' he told me and warned that this is a difficult area for retail investors, who should take the help of a professional in making investment decisions.

Similarly, investing directly in international stocks is a difficult area and Suresh prefers mutual funds that invest internationally. 'International investment is simpler this way and tax treatment after thirty-six months is similar to debt funds,' he told me. But Suresh is against investment in cryptocurrency. 'There is a lot of interest given the fantastic returns in the past. However, information is scarce, there is no regulatory authority, and there is no underlying basis to value it. It is too volatile and goes up and down without any consistent logic. It is best avoided till there is more clarity and some stability is seen there,' he said as we wrapped up our conversation.

6

Checklists for My Money

My gratitude and appreciation to Rohit Shah, principal officer at GYR Financial Planners Private Limited, for helping me in this chapter. Rohit has founded this SEBI-registered investment adviser (registration: INA000015996) company. Rohit is on the board of the Association of Registered Investment Advisers (ARIA) as a director. Before setting up GYR in 2012, Rohit worked extensively at large companies like IBM, Citigroup and Sterlite. The team at GYR has self-published a delightful book, *Money Masters: Stories to Make Kids Money Smart*. You can know more about Rohit and reach out to him via his website: https://www.gettingyourich.com.

A: A Checklist of Basic Financial Products

Note: Each of these products deserves a chapter on its own and summarizing everything into a checklist is only to keep you focused on major points. Financial products have extensive terms and conditions that we agree to comply with when signing on. The nasty surprises come later, so get as much information as you can before committing to invest. There is no guarantee that these products will work for you, so please consult a financial adviser before taking any decision.

Financial product	General guidelines	Fine print
Bank account	Bank charges, range of products and service are more important than the rate of savings bank interest.	Hidden bank charges related to investments, foreign exchange transactions, etc. Be wary of your relationship manager (RM) selling high commission products.
Emergency corpus	Minimum six months of expenses, accessible at (max) twenty-four hours' withdrawal.	To be parked in high-quality fixed deposits or carefully chosen liquid mutual funds.
Credit cards	Look for wide acceptability, low annual fees/lifetime free, low interest rate, and good reward points.	Always pay your dues in full on or before due date, use the cash withdrawal facility only as last resort/emergency and repay the withdrawn amount as soon as possible, always know the cancellation procedure for the card.

Financial product	General guidelines	Fine print
Health insurance	Check your specific medical needs, have adequate cover, have a separate plan over and above what your employer provides you.	Exclusions, waiting periods, room rent limits, fill up your proposal form in all honesty, never hide any detail, pay your premiums on time.
Life insurance	Calculate your cover carefully, reassess your cover every year, customize your policy, consider comprehensive coverage instead of add-ons.	Talk to an adviser. Read and understand the policy before filling, declare every detail in honesty, appoint nominee for every policy. Do not mix investment and insurance.
Equity brokerage	Check range and quality of services and execution, research (if required), and commissions and costs charged.	Unsolicited tips, power of attorneys to control your account, assured return schemes. Regularly check your Demat statements.
Equity mutual funds	Check whether regular or direct scheme, dividend or growth scheme, total expense ratio; check if scheme philosophy and fund manager track record are aligned with your goals and check the riskometer.	Consider index funds and have a long-term plan aligned to your goals.

Financial product	General guidelines	Fine print
Debt mutual funds	Understand concepts of duration, interest rate risk, credit rate risk, defaults, etc.; check the riskometer, align the fund scheme with your goals.	Consider passive debt funds and be clear on the objectives of and expectations from debt funds.

A common question on the financial products listed above is how many should we own. That is, how many bank accounts should we maintain, or how many credit cards should we have, how many stocks should we keep in our portfolio, etc. There is no standard answer to these questions. Have as many as you are comfortable with and can keep track of without losing sleep and peace of mind. The point of owning financial products is not to get the highest possible return, but to give you the best possible comfort when you need it the most. Your credit card is useless if it gets you very high rewards but isn't accepted at a hospital when you need it the most. When you retire, the total quantum of your corpus will matter more to you than whether you beat Warren Buffett. The interest on your savings bank account is pointless if the bank goes under. So, do not yield to peer pressure, do not chase returns without considering risks, and do not do things because you are bored and need excitement in life. There are people who can manage more than five credit cards because they want to maximize reward points. There are people who have thirty to forty stocks and/or equity mutual funds to maximize returns. Many people do many things and just because it works well for them, it does not mean it will work for you. Do not go by what they do. Understand your life and your commitments and plan your finances accordingly.

B: Questions to Ask Before You Commit to an Investment

Here are some checklist questions to help you while making your investments and while choosing a good adviser.

No.	Questions	Response
1	Do you have an emergency corpus in place?	
2	Have you invested the requisite amount to claim your annual tax savings?	
3	Do you have your (and your loved ones') health and life insurance plans in place?	
4	Why do you want to invest? (Because why is more important than what.)	
5	How are you going to manage and monitor this investment?	
6	Who is advising you on this investment? Who are the people behind the investment?	
7	Would you be comfortable if the value drops 30 per cent within six months of your investment?	
8	Is this a regulated investment? If not, then have you considered the impact of the government regulating the investment?	
9	If the returns promised are very high, then have you thought about the capital risk?	
10	Do you understand how the underlying investment makes money for you? For example, if this is a real estate investment, do you understand how commercial/residential real estate works? If this is a stock trading scheme, do you know how trading systems work?	

No.	Questions	Response
11	Is the proposed investment in line with your risk appetite?	
12	Will this investment help you meet your life goals?	
13	If you are going to commit a sizable investment, have you discussed this with your spouse, and if so, are both of you in agreement?	
14	Have you checked all the costs of the product, such as annual maintenance costs, cost of an early exit, cost of liquidation, etc.?	
15	Do you have adequate liquidity for goals maturing in the next three to four years?	
16	Do you understand the cash flows of the investment?	
17	If this is a hybrid product (e.g., ULIP with both insurance and investment) have you tried looking at the underlying assets separately?	
18	If you are investing in a complex, high-yield debt product, do you understand the concept of credit risk?	
19	How liquid is this investment? If there are lock-ins, are you comfortable with freezing up your money, and do you have access to money from other sources if required?	
20	How frequently will the investment value be reported to you?	
21	Will you be able to monitor and review this investment like the rest of your financial portfolio on a single screen? Or will this require a separate monitoring and accounting process?	

No.	Questions	Response
22	Have you thought about concepts of asset allocation, rebalancing and global diversification before making this commitment?	

C: Questions to Ask before Hiring a SEBI-Registered Investment Adviser

No.	Question	Response
1	Have you outlined specific areas in your life on which you need help from the adviser? In case you are meeting the RIA only to get the highest return on your portfolio, please reconsider.	
2	Would you be willing to accept the adviser's recommendations, even if they go against your own preferences?	
3	Is fee income the only source of income for the RIA? For example, will the adviser earn any income from the execution of your plan or from referring you to a third party?	
4	Does the RIA expect that you bring along your spouse/partner or family member to understand your financial needs?	
5	Is the adviser ready for a reference check with a few of his or her existing clients?	
6	What is the RIA's research methodology and investment philosophy for different asset classes that he/she is recommending to you?	
7	Does the adviser have a team? If so, how many people and what are their qualifications?	

No.	Question	Response
8	Can this adviser be a one-stop shop for all your personal finance needs (for example, goals, SIPs, income tax returns, insurance monitoring, drafting of wills, etc.)?	
9	How much time will he/she offer you during a year of engagement? How frequent will the meetings be, and what are the resources the RIA is willing to commit to you?	
10	How accessible is the RIA to you, i.e., will he/she give you an unscheduled and impromptu meeting or call if you need help urgently? Are they or their team members available to answer your questions on email/WhatsApp?	
11	If you decide to terminate the services of the RIA, do they have a well-defined offboarding process to transition out your business?	

D: Sample Financial Plan

A financial plan is central to your financial goals. Having a financial plan and sticking to your discipline over the long term will play a much bigger role in your life than the rate of return on your portfolio. A financial plan also evolves over time. For example, your financial plan when you start your career at age twenty-five will be much simpler than at age thirty-five, when you're married and have kids. Financial plans also have limitations. For example, they are linear while life is full of unexpected events. Think of your financial plan as a guide that will help you plan indulgences like a foreign vacation as well as chalk out a roadmap for a safe and enjoyable retirement. So, spend time on your plan. Early in life, you might want to go the DIY route, but as you progress through life, you might need a financial adviser to help you. The financial plans given below are rough indications to help you understand the basics. In case you'd like to know more, please do reach out to Rohit Shah on his website: https://www.gettingyourich.com.

Basics of a Financial Plan

Risk assessment: Financial plans don't start with numbers. They start with a comprehensive assessment of your risk profile to understand your risk/return expectations, how important are factors like liquidity, stability, volatility, your definition of short-term, long-term, etc., in the way you handle your finances.

Financial position: Think of this as your balance sheet. It's best to include every detail while listing your financial position. This includes every component of income, expenses, assets, liabilities, net worth and insurance. You can then work out your asset allocation across various assets and identify strengths, weaknesses, starting points, etc.

Income, expenditure, savings: Think of this as your profit and loss account. This statement will give you a clear idea of how much you are currently saving and, more importantly, understand where your expenditure is going. For example, look closely at your credit card statements to understand the difference between necessity and indulgence. Your savings depend on your income and expenditure, so you should have a very clear grip on how both these items trend and move in your life.

Insurance and emergency corpus: Having adequate insurance (health and life) and an emergency corpus are critical aspects of your financial planning process. These should be factored into your plan before you define your goals.

Goal planning: This is an important step to understand your aspirations and goals in life. You should include short-term and long-term goals and everything that has a meaningful impact on your cashflows. Longer-term and major goals include retirement, buying a home, educating your children, etc. Short-term goals include buying a car, going on foreign vacations, etc.

Investment planning: Once the goals are defined and your monthly cashflows calculated, you will then find it easier to plan your investments. These investments should be planned keeping your risk/return profile in mind.

Progress and review: Once the financial plan has been implemented, you should track the progress every three to six months at the start. Do not check your portfolio value every day the stock market is open. Remember that the financial plan is a guide to your life, and not to make you a slave. Reviews will help you stay on track and course-correct in case of variations.

We provide two case studies to help you understand the math behind planning for goals. The case studies are not comprehensive financial plans; they are calculations to show you the moving parts in a financial plan. For example, how much should you save to meet a long-term goal, what is the impact of inflation on your planning, etc. Use the case studies as a starting point rather than a definitive guide because each financial plan should be catered to specific needs.

Disclaimer: For the sake of simplicity, both plans do not factor in taxation, do not have detailed income or expense breakdown, ignore decisions like buying/renting a home, exclude provident fund corpus, exclude the creation of an emergency corpus etc.—all of which can significantly change financial plans. To repeat: the idea is to make you focus on the math, not the exact detailing. Once you understand the math, you can easily factor in the above points in your plan.

Case Study 1: Financial Freedom by Forty

In this case study, we take the most popular trend among youth these days, namely financial freedom (FF) at forty. We define financial freedom as having enough corpus at forty to maintain your lifestyle for the rest of your life (till, say, age eighty-five). We take the fictitious example of one Sanjay Gupta, aged twenty-five. We assume that Sanjay completed his graduation at age twenty-one, worked for two years, and then did his two-year full-time MBA. At age twenty-five, he is ready to start his career. For the sake of simplicity, we assume Sanjay will stay single and have no dependents till age forty.

Case Summary

Name	Sanjay Gupta
Age	25
Salary gross	Rs 7 lakh
Salary net	Rs 5.6 lakh
Goal	Financial freedom at forty

Recommendations: Save at least half your salary till the age of forty, invest 70 per cent in equity and 30 per cent in debt. This will give you a corpus of Rs 1.7 crore by age forty. Post-forty, maintain a 50–50 debt/equity till age eighty-five. Here is a summary of our assumptions and recommendations:

Name	Sanjay Gupta
Age at start of financial plan (years)	25
Take home salary (per month)	Rs 46,667
Monthly expenses (50 per cent of salary)	Rs 23,333
Monthly savings (50 per cent of salary)	Rs 23,333
Target age to achieve goal (years)	40
Life expectancy (years)	85
Financial planning period	15 years: 2023 to 2037 (pre-FF) 45 years: 2038 to 2082 (post-FF)
Salary growth	7.85 per cent per annum
Inflation	6.00 per cent
Pre-FF portfolio asset allocation	70 per cent equity, 30 per cent debt
Post-FF portfolio asset allocation	50 per cent equity, 50 per cent debt
Target rate of return (pre-financial freedom)	11.70 per cent (15 per cent on equity, 4 per cent on debt)
Target rate of return (post-financial freedom)	9.00 per cent (14 per cent on equity, 4 per cent on debt)
Target corpus at age 40	Rs 1.74 crore

An easy way to understand this financial plan is as follows:

Current age	25
Target age	40
Target savings	50 per cent of salary
Starting savings/month	Rs 23,333
Required rate of return	11.7 per cent per annum
Salary increase	7.85 per cent per annum
Corpus accumulated at target age	Rs 1.74 crore

The retirement corpus of Rs 1.74 crore should be enough to support his estimated monthly expenses for the rest of his life (assumed till age eighty-five). To repeat our disclaimer: these expenses do not include any provisions for real-life situations like medical emergencies, etc. As we had stated, this example is to explain the math and basic assumptions. In case readers do not agree with any of the assumptions, they can develop and customize a plan for themselves in Microsoft Excel using the future value (FV) and present value (PV) functions as given in the tables below. Readers can use this table and play with the assumptions on savings rate, portfolio returns, etc., to get a better idea of retirement calculators.

Table A: Calculation of Expenses in the Year 2037 (After Inflation)

Age today	A	25
Age of retirement	B	40
Rate of inflation	C	6 per cent (rate)
Number of years	A-B	15 (nper)
Monthly expenses	D	Rs 23,333 (pmt)
Future Value (FV) Formula		=FV (6 per cent,15,0,-23333)
Result (monthly expenses at age 40)	E	Rs 55,920

Table B: Estimating the Corpus Required at Age Forty Till Eighty-Five (2037 to 2082)

Life expectancy	F	85
Portfolio rate of return post retirement	G	9 per cent
Difference between portfolio return and inflation	(1+G/1+C)-1	2.83% which is (1+9%/1+6%)-1 (rate)
Number of years	F-B	45 (nper)
Annual expenses	E x 12	Rs 6,71,036 (pmt)
Present value formula		=PV (2.83%,45,-671036,0,1)
Result (financial freedom corpus based on expense)		Rs 1,74,36,776

Case Study 2: Retirement at Age Sixty-Five

For the second case study, we look at Anchal Singh, age thirty-five. She works as a vice president at a large company and has a salary of Rs 25 lakh. She has two goals—saving about Rs 1.2 crore (in today's value it will be about Rs 2.5 crore when her daughter turns eighteen) to provide for undergraduate studies for her five-year-old daughter and a reasonably good retirement corpus to maintain her lifestyle till the age of eighty-five, which is the estimated life expectancy. Anchal saves a third of her salary and has a taxation rate of 30 per cent. Anchal has a starting corpus of Rs 10 lakh, half of which is parked in FDs and half in an under-construction project that her friend promised was the sweetest real estate deal in Mumbai. The project is currently stuck and has no visibility of execution. Again, for the sake of simplicity, we stick to planning for Anchal's goals and not her family goals.

Case Summary

Name	Anchal Singh
Age	35
Salary gross	Rs 25 lakh
Salary net	Rs 17.5 lakh
Starting corpus	Rs 10 lakh (Rs 5 lakh in a real estate project, Rs 5 lakh in an FD)
Goals	Retirement corpus for self, based on expenses Education corpus in 2035, when daughter turns 18

Recommendations:

a) Take back the Rs 5 lakh security deposit from the real estate builder and liquidate the fixed deposit of Rs 5 lakh and invest as given in the next point.

b) Maintain a 30 per cent savings rate. Until retirement (age 65), invest 60 per cent in equities and 40 per cent in debt. At age sixty-five, invest 40 per cent in equity and 60 per cent in debt.

c) When your daughter turns eighteen in the year 2035, withdraw Rs 2.50 crore from the corpus.

d) At age sixty-five, your retirement corpus will amount to Rs 11.35 crore, which will be enough to sustain your monthly expenses, factoring in inflation.

Here is a summary of our assumptions and recommendations:

Name	Anchal Singh
Age at start of the financial plan (years)	35
Take-home salary (per month)	Rs 1,45,833
Monthly expenses (67 per cent of salary)	Rs 97,708
Monthly savings (33 per cent of salary)	Rs 48,125
Target age to achieve goal (years)	65
Life expectancy (years)	85
Financial planning period	30 years: 2023 to 2052 (working career) 20 years: 2053 to 2072 (retirement and later)

Name	Anchal Singh
Salary growth	7.17 per cent per annum
Inflation	6 per cent
Pre-retirement portfolio asset allocation	60 per cent equity, 40 per cent debt
Post-retirement portfolio asset allocation	40 per cent equity, 60 per cent debt
Target rate of return (pre-financial freedom)	10.6 per cent (15 per cent on equity, 4 per cent on debt)
Target rate of return (post-financial freedom)	8 per cent (14 per cent on equity, 4 per cent on debt)
Target corpus at age 65	Rs 11.34 crore
Actual accumulated corpus at age 65	Rs 11.54 crore

As given in Case Study 1, here are the Excel calculations behind the main numbers:

Table A: Calculation of Expenses in the Year 2052 (After Inflation)

Age today	A	35
Age of retirement	B	65
Rate of inflation	C	6 per cent (rate)
Number of years	A-B	30 (nper)
Monthly expenses	D	Rs 97,708 (pmt)
Future Value (FV) Formula		=FV (6%,30,0,-97,708)
Result (monthly expenses at age 40)	E	Rs 5,61,187

Table B: Estimating the Corpus Required at Age Forty Till Eighty-Five (2052 to 2072)

Life expectancy	F	85
Portfolio rate of return (post retirement)	G	8 per cent
Difference between portfolio return and inflation	(1+G/1+C)-1	1.89 per cent which is (1+8%/1+6%)-1 (rate)
Number of years	F-B	20 (nper)
Annual expenses	Ex12	Rs 67,34,243 (pmt)
Present value formula		=PV (1.89%,20,-6734243,,1)
Result (financial freedom corpus based on expense)		Rs 11,34,27,562

Notes on the Assumptions

The plans given above are purely hypothetical, whereas real life, obviously, is much more complex and nuanced. All the financial discipline in the world goes for a toss if stock markets don't deliver as per our estimates. Medical emergencies can, unfortunately, wipe out years of savings. The purpose of a financial plan is to equip you for your goals and keep you on track to achieve them. Some of our assumptions might seem generous to some readers and miserly to others. There may be some who want to retire early and want a minimalist lifestyle. There are others who want a more lavish lifestyle. Hence, the objections to our assumptions can be endless. In our defence, what we want to convey in our case studies are the following points that will not change with any assumptions:

1. Financial plans are financial statements of our lives, namely: profit and loss, balance sheet and cashflow. Preparing and reviewing them every year should be part of your discipline.
2. Your discipline in sticking to a plan will matter more than how the stock market does every year. Whether you beat the best investors is meaningless.
3. Financial plans are based on input and output. Hence, there are only a few variables in your control within a financial plan, namely, your goals and your savings rate. These two variables will help you with your asset allocation.
4. And finally, focus on increasing your income by investing in yourself, staying in good health (physically and mentally), and achieving your targets. For more, do read *The Victory Project*.

Adviser Perspectives: Vishal and Shalini Dhawan

SEBI registration number: INA000000409
Website: https://planahead.in/

Vishal and Shalini Dhawan have degrees in business management and met each other for the first time during their management studies at Welingkar Institute of Management, Mumbai, in the mid-1990s. After various jobs in their early career, they started Plan Ahead in 2003. Since then, Plan Ahead has grown to be an award-winning, leading, full-service, fee-only financial advisory firm. Vishal holds CFP certification from FPSB India and is a licensed financial life planner from Money Quotient (USA). Vishal is also active in the RIA industry—he is a founding member and vice chairman of ARIA (Association of Registered Investment Advisers) and was the chair of the International Knowledge Circle at the Financial Planning Association, USA, in 2014. Shalini holds a life planning certificate on the Seven Stages of Money Maturity from the Kinder Institute of Life Planning, USA. Shalini is also from the 2011 cohort of the ISB Goldman Sachs 10000 Women Entrepreneurship Program.

Plan Ahead was the Gold Award winner for the Best RIA in India, from 2016 to 2019, at the Outlook Money Awards.

I spoke with Vishal and Shalini on 22 October 2021 on a Zoom call, and these are the highlights of our conversation.

Vishal and Shalini knew early on that they would start their own firm. While both met in B-school for the first time, they went through different careers before narrowing their venture's idea to financial advisory. Vishal's last job was at the wealth management team at ABN AMRO in Delhi, and Shalini, who followed Vishal to Delhi from Mumbai, last worked for Ernst & Young. In 2003, they moved back to Mumbai to start Plan Ahead. Why did they leave their cushy jobs at large organizations to enter the nascent field of financial planning?

'After working in financial services for seven years, I realized that there was no independent, holistic advice to help us understand the trade-offs involved in making major life decisions—like leaving your job and starting your own venture. The idea came to us a year before we cut the cord and started preparing for it by taking certain decisions like not buying a house, rationalizing our lifestyle, etc.,' Vishal told me.[1]

How do Vishal and Shalini divide their roles at Plan Ahead? 'Two things we both spend time on are clients and products. Beyond that, I handle research and media appearances, while Shalini handles operations, marketing, IT, HR, etc.,' Vishal told me. There are instances when Vishal and Shalini differ and these instances are typically about investment vehicles versus goals; for example, Vishal would like an investment product because it looks good from a risk-adjusted return perspective, but Shalini might have a different point of view looking at the relevance of the products, given the client's goals. However, they agree that every step that they take for their client families should add meaning to their client's finances and time to their client's life.

Evolution of Financial Planning

As we begin our conversation on financial planning, I asked Vishal and Shalini how financial planning has evolved over the years. Shalini told me, 'When we started off in 2003, we were learners. Over time and as we interacted with more clients, the biggest learning was that we needed to spend more time understanding the main part of the plan—the client. It's so much more about the client than it is about the money. Now, a lot of our work starts with deep conversations with the client's family that we have taken specific coaching in, as both of us are financial life planners.[2] We've gained many insights along the way. For example, one insight was that transitions in life are very important, such as transition from work to retirement, transitioning a child from school to college, etc. These transitions require us to guide our clients. Another insight was the importance of family—that's an area where our (India) needs were very different from the USA (some of our tools are licensed from the USA). For example, we have conversations with both spouses. In some cases, we found that the wife chose to become a homemaker after a very successful career and (after her kids were grown up) wanted to start working again. So then, as planners, we needed to enable the set-up of a business for her and that gives a whole new dimension to the plan.'

Financial Planning for Women

I asked Shalini how financial planning for women has changed over the years. 'Today, we have more women entrepreneurs and more financial products. So back then (in 2003), women would invest their money in FDs, whereas now they are leading conversations with us on money and finance. Previously, we insisted that clients get their wives along but now it's not so much of an effort. There is also more acceptance in society of divorce, single mothers, separation, widows, etc. These transitions are making women think about money, which was earlier done by the spouse. Now women need to look at this closely and ask themselves questions like, how do I take decisions for my child if I'm separated? As we mature as a society and become more accepting of live-ins, divorce, separation, LGBT couples, etc., there will be more openness to meet advisers as you head towards these events in life. And finally, the last couple of years have taught people that life can be fragile, and they need to connect with their spouse especially on money matters,' Shalini told me.

Shalini also believes that the current set of financial products are good enough for women. 'What needs to be improved is education for women, in order to make them more involved in the financial planning process. Statistically, women live longer than men, so women should not stay out (or be kept out) of the financial planning process with their spouses. Financial planners also need to approach women with empathy rather than sympathy, which includes empathy towards the life-stage (in terms of career, family, marital status, responsibility of children, etc.) and the risk profile (conservative, aggressive, etc.) of women,' she said.

Common Misconceptions about Financial Planning

What were some of the most common misconceptions that they observed in their clients when it came to investments? Vishal said, 'The most common one is that the difference between success and failure is the rate of return on my investment portfolio. It's not. The difference between success and failure is your rate of savings. Instead of craving for 15 per cent per year, we suggest why not save, say, Rs 50,000 more per year? That's when the conversation takes a different direction. The second misconception is that India is the hottest (investment) market. Long-term data doesn't support that and in fact, India is where there is higher volatility. As per actual data, India is somewhere in middle (in terms of stock market returns). So, we encourage our clients to have exposure to an international portfolio. And the third misconception is that financial planning is only about achieving goals. Our view is that financial planning is about planning multiple scenarios, because there is no way to know the future and how your life will pan out. So, if you want to plan these scenarios, you plan them in peacetime, not in wartime. Don't sit and plan when you've lost your job. You need to plan for that job loss in advance and know exactly what you want to be able to do when you lose your job. So, it's not just about Plan A, it's about having thought about Plan B, Plan C and Plan D.'

Importance of Financial Planning

We spoke about how financial planning helps people take the right decisions at critical junctures, and Vishal narrated an interesting case study. A client who is a successful doctor and ran his nursing home wanted to expand and set up a hospital. 'So, we did what we always do—opened an MS Excel worksheet, plugged in capital expenditure, budgeted revenues, costs, timelines, and built a mathematical model to calculate the break-even point of the project. But our licensed life planning tools helped us have deeper conversations. In the early days of our engagement, we figured that travel and photography were two passions that consumed him. So, we told him that he can invest in the hospital, but he would no longer be able to take his habitual two months off in a year to travel. For that to happen, he'd have to get in a partner into the hospital. Was he willing to make this trade-off between his passion and ambition? We told him that this decision had to be taken before making the investment decision. He thought about it and eventually came back to us saying that he would stick to his nursing home,' Vishal said.

Shalini explained that these tools (licensed from Money Quotient and George Kinder) gave clients a lot of space (in the form of detailed answers) to express their deepest values and most cherished things in lives and help Vishal and Shalini to map out the appropriate financial solutions aligned to these values—instead of restricting solutions to what an MS Excel sheet throws up.

As we ended the interview, I posed the most commonly asked questions to Vishal and Shalini, and these are their answers:

- How does a beginner start to learn about managing his money? Shalini pointed to Plan Ahead's blog on their website (planahead.in) and Plan Ahead's YouTube channel (URL: https://www.youtube.com/user/PlanAheadIndia/videos). She also suggested the National Centre for Financial Education's website (ncfe.org.in) which has a wealth of resources and information, including a section on financial planning, and is ideal for beginners.

- What are the basic financial products that everyone should consider? Vishal lists them as 1) independent term insurance (over and above the one provided by your employer, if applicable) if you have dependents, 2) independent health insurance policy (in addition to what is provided by your employer), 3) bank deposits or liquid funds to cover for emergency provisions, 4) index funds to participate in India as well as overseas equity opportunities, and 5) instruments dedicated towards your retirement savings; these could include PPF, NPS but not insurance policies that are sold as retirement products.

- Stocks versus mutual funds: Mutual funds over stocks. Vishal and Shalini believe that asset allocation starts with geography and not asset class. So, they don't agree with a portfolio that consists of, say, equities, bonds, real estate, FDs, provident funds—all in India. Stocks are valuable if you have a very well-defined strategy such as large-cap stocks that have fallen out of favour. But you can't run a stock portfolio with a strategy that first asks what's the best mid-cap or small-cap stock to buy today and then goes on to hold on to those stocks for the long term.

- Active versus passive: Data now suggests that passive works in India. Vishal and Shalini believe that the active part of portfolios should be satellite and passive part should be core—a few years ago, it was the reverse. So now, if there are specific opportunities in the market, then active is good. Otherwise, stick with passive—the costs of both products are insanely different. As they said, 'We build the domestic part of the passive portfolio using Nifty 50 index funds and for international exposure, we use a similar mix of MSCI World index funds and S&P 500 index funds. There might also be specific opportunities that we participate in, and for that, we use factor-based or smart beta solutions on a tactical basis.'

- Rent or buy a house: 'The first thing to ask is whether this is a financial decision or a core value decision. If it is purely a financial decision, there is enough evidence to show that renting a house is far more attractive because of its flexibility in terms of choice; renting also suits certain phases of life, say, when you're younger and want to be an entrepreneur and don't want to commit to a home loan. But when you have settled down (which happens at different points for different people), we think that buying the one house that you're going to live in is a good idea even if it's not the best financial decision. So, as long as you are clear about affordability, about funding it intelligently and not going over the top (like making it the status symbol in your life), we are very comfortable with people having a primary residence that they own. We even suggest that professionals should own their primary office as well, because time is important to them and what you don't want to do is spend inordinate time in shifting offices.'

- FDs and debt funds: Tax is the biggest differentiator. For those in a low tax bracket, FDs make sense and for those in a high tax bracket, debt funds are better. For beginners in a high tax bracket, it makes sense to start in FDs and—as you learn more and get comfortable with the products—move towards debt funds.

- International investing and cryptocurrency: 'As per recent SEBI norms, we are not allowed to recommend products that are not regulated. Irrespective of that, we don't recommend cryptocurrency because we are not convinced about the utility/use cases and the valuation parameters of this vehicle. We do recommend international investments and prefer passive products for this purpose.'

- Five questions to ponder while choosing a financial adviser.

  o What is his or her experience of dealing with bull markets and bear markets?

  o What license does the adviser have and how does he/she earn his/her revenues?

  o What are the conversations the adviser is having with me and how well does he/she understand me?

  o Can the adviser offer multi-product advice and explain why and how these products are relevant to me?

  o How does the adviser stay current in terms of their skill, and how does the adviser help me stay current with my financial goals?

Acknowledgements

My gratitude to the front-line and health-care workers, doctors and medical staff, to the police, to municipal workers, to the delivery riders, and everyone who ensured that 'normal' was possible during the worst parts of the pandemic. I can't name all of them who helped because I wouldn't even know who they are. But all of them helped to make things 'normal' enough for me at home to write this book.

Thanks to everyone at home who helped this giant ship of a book to sail. So, thanks to my mother, Shubhra Saran, my wife, Vanita, and my son, Varun. Thanks to my sister, Rashmi, her husband, Tarun, and their children, Amrita and Smriti, for the encouragement, coffees and dinners to pull me through writer's block. Writing a book isn't easy but handling me and my various mood swings for more than a year while writing my first solo book was a thankless task for which no amount of gratitude from me is enough.

Thanks to Saurabh Mukherjea of Marcellus for his endless help, ideas and constant support, quite literally from when this book started as a four-page proposal to Penguin. It is an honour to have Saurabh write the foreword to this book. My work with Saurabh, from his days at Ambit Capital to *The Unusual Billionaires* and finally to *The Victory Project*, constituted the best moments in my professional career so far. His belief in my ability to write remains a source of motivation for me. I remain grateful to my ex-boss Anirudha Dutta for introducing me to Saurabh back in 2013; this book would not have existed if it hadn't been for that introduction.

My gratitude to the team at Penguin Random House India for bringing this book to life. Thanks to Manish Kumar at PRHI for commissioning this book. I worked with Manish for *The Victory Project: Six Steps to Peak Potential* (authored by Saurabh Mukherjea and co-authored by me, 2020) and his energy, enthusiasm and efforts (despite being down with COVID-19 in 2021) are the main reasons why this book has seen the light of day. Thanks to the brilliant and meticulous copy editors Sundeep Tampa and Vineet Gill, for hand-holding me through the copy-editing and proofreading processes. They provided much-needed clarity of thought to lift the text from many muddled moments in the original manuscript. Thanks to Sanchita Mukherjee for thinking up and designing the cover of this book.

Thanks to Monika Halan for her guidance, help and advice for this book. Monika introduced me to Deepti Bhaskaran, and I am very grateful to Deepti for providing me with the foundation and direction of what would become the RIA survey and the RIA questionnaires. This book has benefited tremendously from her experience and insights.

Once the methodology for the RIA survey was finalized, I sent out emails to around 1300 SEBI RIAs for the purposes of this book and my thanks to each and every one who replied. My thanks to the shortlisted RIAs who took the time to reply to the detailed questionnaires sent to them. Thanks (in alphabetical order of first name) to Dilshad Billimoria, Harsh Roongta, Lovaii Navlakhi, Melvin Joseph, Suresh Sadagopan,

Vishal and Shalini Dhawan for being generous with their time in answering the questionnaires and then for the interviews that are part of this book. Thanks to Rohit Shah for the detailed work on the final chapter. This book stands on the insights, advice and valuable perspectives that they were all kind enough to share with me.

Thanks to Professor Pattabiraman (*Freefincal*), Ashal Jauhari (ASAN Ideas for Wealth), Sadique Neelgund (Network FP), and Kayezad Adajania (Moneycontrol) for their time in replying in detail to my questionnaires and for the Zoom calls. My thanks to Kalpen Parekh and Arun Rajendran of DSP Mutual Fund, and Aashish P. Somaiyaa of White Oak. I am grateful for their support.

Thanks (in alphabetical order of first name) to Deepak Shenoy of CapitalMind, Devang Shah of Right Returns, Jinay Savla of Circle Wealth Advisors, Mahavir Chopra of Beshak, Ronak Hindocha of IFANow and Shweta Jain of Investography for their guidance in helping me understand the world of RIAs. Thanks to Erik Hon of iFast for his support, insights and for introducing me to the right people. Thanks to Avinash Luthria of Fiduciaries for his patience and his time for our detailed discussions on the finer aspects of RIAs.

My thanks to Amit Doshi and Kavita Rajwade of IVM Podcasts (now part of Pratilipi). Our podcast *Paisa Vaisa* was born from a completely random meeting at his studio in Khar in 2017. *Paisa Vaisa* was named after an obscure song from the 1990s, and neither Amit nor I knew that it would go where it did—five years, a million-plus listens, 350 episodes, 150 guests and counting. Thanks to everyone at Team IVM for working hard and producing a podcast that both of us are proud of and for managing a very grouchy host. And finally, thanks to all the listeners of the *Paisa Vaisa* podcast—thank you for listening, for your support and for giving me the idea for this book.

Notes

Preface

1. Source: Zerodha, https://zerodha.com/z-connect/featured/broking-goes-mainstream-dec-2021, last accessed on 13 February 2022.
2. Details here: https://www.imdb.com/title/tt12392504/, last accessed on 13 February 2022.
3. Available here: https://www.sebi.gov.in/sebiweb/other/OtherAction.do?doRecognisedFpi=yes&intmId=13

Chapter 1: A Brave New World

1. Refer to the circular here: https://www.sebi.gov.in/legal/circulars/jun-2001/index-based market-wide-circuit-breaker-in-compulsory-rolling-settlement_17986.html, last accessed 8 February 2022.
2. Source: https://www.livemint.com/news/india/more-than-50-of-india-s-population-25-yrs-or-older-survey-11593793054491.html, last accessed 7 February 2022.
3. Available here: https://www.icicisecurities.com/Upload/ArticleAttachments/ICICI_Securities_Limited_Annual_Report_FY2020_21.pdf, last accessed 8 February 2022.

4. Available here: https://zerodha.com/z-connect/featured/broking-goes-mainstream-dec-2021, last accessed 9 February 2022.

5. Available here: https://pib.gov.in/PressReleaseIframePage.aspx?PRID=1780999, last accessed 9 February 2022.

6. Available here: https://www.sebi.gov.in/reports-and-statistics/publications/jan-2022/sebi-bulletin-january-2022_55591.html, last accessed 9 February 2022.

7. Data source: https://www.amfiindia.com/Themes/Theme1/downloads/home/FolioandTicketSize.pdf, last accessed 9 February 2022.

8. Available here: https://www.amfiindia.com/mutual-fund, last accessed 9 February 2022.

9. Available here: https://www.indiabudget.gov.in/economicsurvey/, last accessed 9 February 2022.

10. Available here: https://www.sbimf.com/en-us/other-schemes/sbi-etf-nifty-50, last accessed 10 February 2022.

11. Available here: https://m.rbi.org.in/scripts/FAQView.aspx?Id=115#Q1, last accessed 10 February 2022.

12. Available here: https://www.reddit.com/r/wallstreetbets/, last accessed 16 May 2022.

13. https://www.indiadatahub.com/insights/article/the-big-small-savings

14. Source, AMFI: https://www.amfiindia.com/indian-mutual, last accessed 11 February 2022.

Chapter 2: *Kal, Aaj Aur Kal*

1. Available here: https://twitter.com/elonmusk/status/1276418907968925696?, last accessed 3 February 2022.

2. Available here: https://www.buzzfeed.com/sumedha_bharpilania/indian-parent-memes, last accessed 3 February 2022.

3. Available here: https://twitter.com/thenikhilkapur/status/1026533277123788801, last accessed 3 February 2022.
4. Available here: https://tvfplay.com/show/tech-conversations-with/6, last accessed 4 February 2022.
5. Source: BSE: https://www.bseindia.com/static/about/History_Milestones.html, last accessed 5 February 2022.
6. Source: RBI data available here: https://www.rbi.org.in/scripts/PublicationsView.aspx?id=12765, last accessed 4 February 2022.
7. Available here: https://icrier.org/pdf/wp91.pdf, last accessed 4 February 2022.
8. Available here: https://www.linkedin.com/posts/aseem-dhru-2231401_hdfcbank-banking-sbfc-activity-6891198543197978624-FuJm, last accessed 4 February 2022.
9. National Securities Depository Limited (NSDL).
10. News source: https://www.nirmalbang.com/knowledge-center/mutualfund-evolution-in-india.html, last accessed 5 February 2022.
11. News source: https://economictimes.indiatimes.com/mf/analysis/25-years-of-pvt-sector-mutual-funds-major-reforms-in-the-industry/articleshow/65147681.cms, last accessed 5 February 2022.

Adviser Perspectives: Harsh Roongta

1. https://www.forbesindia.com/article/investment-guide-2015/return-is-king-in-real-estate/39453/1

Chapter 3: How Fintechs Changed Personal Finance

1. Available here: https://www.imf.org/external/pubs/ft/fandd/2021/07/india-stack-financial-access-and-digital-inclusion.htm, last accessed 25 January 2022.

2. Available here: https://www.ndtv.com/business/whatsapp-like-movement-in-indian-finance-sector-nandan-nilekani-1209635, last accessed 20 January 2022.

3. Available here: https://youtu.be/aGM5TvAUF00, last accessed 20 January 2022.

4. Available here: https://www.investindia.gov.in/sector/bfsi-fintech-financial-services, last accessed 21 January 2022.

5. Available here: https://nasscom.in/knowledge-center/publications/nasscom-tech-start-report-2021-year-titans, last accessed 21 January 2022.

6. https://timesofindia.indiatimes.com/business/india-business/indians-placed-record-bets-on-us-stocks-in-21/articleshow/89080301.cms

7. Source: Group M: https://www.groupm.com/newsroom/india-influencer-marketing-report/, last accessed 2 February 2022.

8. As per Pew research available here: https://www.pewresearch.org/fact-tank/2019/01/17/where-millennials-end-and-generation-z-begins/, last accessed 2 February 2022.

9. Available here: https://www.facebook.com/groups/asanideasforwealth/about, last accessed 2 February 2022.

10. Stock price as on 3 February 2022, available here: https://www.nseindia.com/get-quotes/equity?symbol=YESBANK

Chapter 4: The FIRE Dream

1. As of 16 May 2022, using a closing Sensex value of 52,974, compared with the closing value of 25,981 on 23 March 2020. On an annualized basis, Sensex has delivered a 39 per cent CAGR over this period. Data available here: https://www.bseindia.com/Indices/IndexArchiveData.html, last accessed 17 May 2022.

2. Available to download and read on HDFC Mutual Fund's website [PDF]: https://files.hdfcfund.com/s3fs-public/2022-01/HDFC%20MF%20Yearbook%202022_2.pdf, last accessed 18 January 2022.
3. https://timesofindia.indiatimes.com/business/india-business/india-to-grow-at-8-5-in-2022-will-retain-fastest-growing-economy-tag-imf/articleshow/86973062.cms
4. World Bank data available here: https://data.worldbank.org/indicator/NY.GDP.PCAP.CD, last accessed 18 January 2022.
5. Available here: https://en.wikipedia.org/wiki/Enquire_Within_upon_Everything, last accessed 20 January 2022.
6. Available here: https://en.wikipedia.org/wiki/FIRE_movement, last accessed 20 January 2022.
7. Available here: https://www.reddit.com/r/financialindependence/, last accessed 20 January 2022.
8. https://www.livemint.com/market/cryptocurrency/crypto-scam-sites-continue-to-draw-indians-in-droves-11642359173649.html

Adviser Perspectives: Vishal and Shalini Dhawan

1. Vishal also referred to his 2012 article on Network FP titled 'Kick Your Corporate Job and Start Your Advisory Practice!': https://networkfp.com/kick-your-corporate-job-and-start-your-advisory-practice/
2. Financial life planners take an approach to financial planning which explores client relationships as a whole and not just by the numbers.

References

Foreword

Marcellus, 26 November 2019, https://marcellus.in/blogs/nifty-indian-gdp-a-complete-breakdown-in-relationship/#

Sunil Dhawan, *Financial Express*, 10 May 2022, https://www.financialexpress.com/money/mutual-funds/all-time-high-sip-accounts-at-5-39-crore-in-april-2022-as-fy-23-starts-with-net-flows-for-mf-schemes/2519230/

Kumar Shankar Roy, Statistalk, *HinduBusinessLine*, 22 March 2022, https://www.thehindubusinessline.com/opinion/columns/statistalk/india-becoming-active-on-passive-mf-investments/article65250068.ece

Deepti Bhaskaran and Monika Halan, Mint Insurance, *Mint*, 12 February 2013, https://www.livemint.com/Money/Bn8wj4mBbZP3hAI0la0sXL/Investors-lost-15-trillion-due-to-insurance-misselling.html

Briefing, *The Economist*, 14 May 2022, https://www.economist.com/briefing/2022/05/14/india-is-likely-to-be-the-worlds-fastest-growing-big-economy-this-year

Chapter 1: A Brave New World

Surajeet Dasgupta, *Mint*, 13 March 2020, https://www.livemint.com/market/stock-market-news/bse-nse-halt-trading-for-first-time-12-years-circuit-breaker-limits-explained-11584071686665.html

Disha Sanghvi, *Mint*, 24 July 2019, https://www.livemint.com/mutual-fund/mf-news/millennials-almost-half-of-new-mutual-fund-investors-in-fy19-1563905268879.html

Economic Times, 3 July 2021, https://economictimes.indiatimes.com/markets/stocks/news/over-70-of-2m-new-customers-first-time-investors-upstox/articleshow/84066974.cms

Nasrin Sultana and Ashwin Ramarathinam, *Mint*, 27 April 2021, https://www.livemint.com/market/stock-market-news/demat-account-openings-hit-a-record-of-14-2-mn-in-fy2021-11619465145852.html

Jash Kripalani, Moneycontrol.com, 15 December 2021, https://www.moneycontrol.com/news/photos/business/personal-finance/five-mutual-funds-that-had-record-collections-during-their-nfos-in-2021-7812951.html

Moneycontrol, 27 August 2021, https://www.moneycontrol.com/news/business/personal-finance/sbi-balanced-advantage-fund-set-to-record-highest-ever-nfo-collection-at-rs-13000-crore-7389491.html

Economic Times, 6 August 2015, https://economictimes.indiatimes.com/industry/banking/finance/epfo-to-invest-nearly-rs-5000-crore-in-stocks-in-2015-16/articleshow/48375783.cms?from=mdr

V. Keshavdev, *Fortune India*, 15 December 2021, https://www.fortuneindia.com/macro/reverse-fdi-indians-transferred-68-billion-overseas-in-5-yrs/106371

Maggie Fitzgerald, CNBC, 12 May 2020, https://www.cnbc. com/2020/05/12/young-investors-pile-into-stocks-seeing-generational-buying-moment-instead-of-risk.html

Shikhar Balwani, Rononjoy Mazumdar and Nupur Acharya, Bloomberg, 24 March 2021, https://www.bloomberg.com/ news/articles/2021-03-23/millions-of-millennials-are-piling-into-india-s-stock-market?sref=Wq5d68P0

Luke Kawa, Bloomberg, 26 February 2020, https://www. bloomberg.com/news/articles/2020-02-26/reddit-s-profane-greedy-traders-are-shaking-up-the-stock-market?sref=Wq5d68P0

Gunjan Banerji, Juliet Chung and Caitlin McCabe, *Wall Street Journal*, 27 January 2021, https://www.wsj.com/articles/ gamestop-mania-reveals-power-shift-on-wall-streetand-the-pros-are-reeling-11611774663

Megha Mandavia, *Economic Times*, 4 February 2021, https:// economictimes.indiatimes.com/tech/technology/ clubhouse-app-lets-do-a-clubhouse-indias-startup-leaders-say/articleshow/80678961.cms?from=mdr

Jeran Wittenstein, Nick Turner and Bloomberg, *Fortune*, 31 January 2022, https://fortune.com/2022/01/21/netflix-peloton-zoom-wocs-end-lockdown-stocks-era-covid/

Oscar Gonsalez, CNET, 29 January 2022, https://www.cnet. com/news/gamestop-what-happened-after-everyday-stock-traders-rocked-wall-street/

Ashutosh Shyam and Rajesh Naidu, *Economic Times*, 11 February 2022, https://economictimes.indiatimes.com/mf/ mf-news/mutual-funds-sip-assets-hit-record-rs-5-8-lakh-cr-in-jan/articleshow/89491026.cms

Abhinav Kaul, Mint, 31 January 2022, https://www. livemint.com/mutual-fund/mf-news/sebi-restricts-overseas-investments-by-mfs-what-should-investors-do-11643617637642.html

RBI, July 2017, https://rbidocs.rbi.org.in/rdocs/Publication
    Report/Pdfs/HFCRA28D0415E2144A009112
    DD314ECF5C07.PDF

Bhupal Singh and Indrajit Roy, RBI, Mint Street Memos,
    11 August 2017, https://www.rbi.org.in/Scripts/MSM_
    Demonetisation.aspx

Manoranjan Dash et al., RBI, Mint Street Memo, August 2011,
    2017, https://www.rbi.org.in/Scripts/MSM_Financial
    isationofSavings.aspx

IndiaDataHub.com, 10 February 2022, https://www.
    indiadatahub.com/insights/article/the-big-small-savings

ET Brand Equity, *Economic Times*, 18 March 2017, https://
    brandequity.economictimes.indiatimes.com/news/
    advertising/mutual-funds-sahi-hai-says-amfi-in-their-
    new-ad-campaign/57701407

ET Brand Equity, *Economic* Times, 15 September 2020,
    https://brandequity.economictimes.indiatimes.com/news/
    marketing/amfi-signs-four-more-cricketers-to-create-
    awareness-around-mutual-funds/78110117

Rachna Monga Koppika, Moneycontrol, 16 December 2020,
    https://www.moneycontrol.com/news/business/personal-
    finance/dilshad-billimoria-on-involving-both-spouses-in-
    a-familys-money-management-decisions-6234401.html

Business Standard, 23 March 2020, https://www.business-
    standard.com/podcast/markets/market-wrap-march-
    23-here-s-all-that-happened-in-the-markets-
    today-120032301143_1.html

Chapter 2: *Kal, Aaj Aur Kal*

Kayezad Adajania, *Mint*, 24 December 2013, https://www.
    livemint.com/Companies/VH3ukPOCTWnyd10FafHsqK/

HDFC-Asset-Management-acquires-Morgan-Stanley-Investments-M.html

Hamish McDonald, *Ambani and Sons: The making of the World's Richest Brothers and Their Feud*, Lotus Collection, Roli Books, 2010.

Gautam Chikermane, *Seventy Policies That Shaped India: 1947 to 2017, Independence to $2.5 Trillion*, Observer Research Foundation, 2018.

R. Balakrishnan, Prime Investor, 23 January 2022, https://primeinvestor.in/interest-rates-should-you-move-out-of-equities/

Ajay Shah and Susan Thomas, ICRIER, https://icrier.org/pdf/wp91.pdf

Vivek Kaul, ET Panache, *Economic Times*, 1 July 2011, https://economictimes.indiatimes.com/master-move-how-dhirubhai-ambani-turned-the-tables-on-the-kolkata-bear-cartel/articleshow/9059587.cms?from=mdr

Saurabh Mukherjea, Moneycontrol, 6 August 2018, https://www.moneycontrol.com/news/business/markets/coffee-can-investing-s-narens-biggest-contrarian-call-betting-his-house-on-a-real-estate-crash 2808101.html

Avneet Kaur, *Economic* Times, 26 July 2018, https://economictimes.indiatimes.com/mf/analysis/25-years-of-pvt-sector-mutual-funds-major-reforms-in-the-industry/articleshow/65147681.cms?from=mdr

Chapter 3: How Fintechs Changed Personal Finance

Mint, 29 July 2019, https://www.livemint.com/companies/start-ups/how-paytm-qr-codes-revolutionised-digital-payments-in-india-1564401824780.html

Jasmeet Singh, Gadgets 360, NDTV.com, 27 December 2017, https://gadgets.ndtv.com/apps/news/paytm-app-100-million-downloads-google-play-1792801

Devina Sengupta and Danish Khan, *Economic Times*, 28 November 2016, https://economictimes.indiatimes.com/news/economy/policy/reliance-jio-crosses-50-million-subscribers-in-83-days/articleshow/55670041.cms

Muntazir Abbas, *Economic Times*, 26 October 2021, https://economictimes.indiatimes.com/news/india/indias-growing-data-usage-smartphone-adoption-to-boost-digital-india-initiatives-top-bureaucrat/articleshow/87275402.cms

Tushar Deep Singh, *Economic Times*. 4 January 2022, https://economictimes.indiatimes.com/tech/tech-bytes/upi-transactions-scale-new-peak-in-december-2021/articleshow/88689479.cms

Sindhu Hariharan, *Times of India*, 24 January 2022, https://timesofindia.indiatimes.com/business/india-business/indians-placed-record-bets-on-us-stocks-in-21/articleshow/89080301.cms

Shubham Raj, ETmarkets.com, *Economic Times*, 10 January 2022, https://economictimes.indiatimes.com/markets/bonds/mutual-fund-sip-contribution-hits-record-rs-11305-crore/articleshow/88815036.cms?from=mdr

Bhumika Khatri and Aishwarya Vishanathan, Ken, 10 December 2021, https://the-ken.com/story/leveraging-likes-for-a-living-inside-indias-rs-900-crore-influencer-economy/

Misyrlena Egkolfopoulou, Bloomberg Wealth, Bloomberg, 17 September 2021, https://www.bloomberg.com/news/articles/2021-09-17/social-media-influencers-income-advertising-wall-street-products?sref=Wq5d68P0

Varsha Santosh and Ami Shah, ET Prime, *Economic Times*, 14 June 2021, https://economictimes.indiatimes.com/ prime/money-and-markets/meet-pattabiraman-the-man-who-helps-many-plan-a-better-retirement-through-his-calculators/primearticleshow/83410086.cms

Darshan Mehta, Bloomberg Quint, 22 August 2019, https:// www.bloombergquint.com/business/what-has-sent-the-yes-bank-stock-into-a-tailspin

Nithin Kamath, Zerodha, 23 August 2019, https://zerodha. com/z-connect/traders-zone/lessons-from-trading-on-yes-bank

Sucheta Dalal, Moneylife, 21 January 2022, https://www. moneylife.in/article/many-ways-of-being-fooled-in-a-bull-market/66172.html

T.E. Narasimhan, *Business Standard*, 17 October 2016, https://www.business-standard.com/article/companies/ gopal-srinivasan-narayan-k-seshadri-others-invest-in-financial-planning-firm-international-money-matters-116101700193_1.html

Priya Ganapati, Rediff, 2 August 2001, https://www.rediff. com/money/2001/aug/02indya.htm

Chapter 4: The FIRE Dream

Moneycontrol, 9 September 2021, https://www.moneycontrol. com/news/business/markets/daily-voice-amar-ambani-of-yes-securities-sees-sensex-at-125000-by-2025-outlook-for-next-4-years-extremely-positive-7445461.html

Press release, Ministry of Statistics and Programmme Implementation, 7 January 2022, https://www.mospi. gov.in/documents/213904/416359//Press%20Note%20 FAE%202021-22m1641557278684.pdf/d4df7f8c-779a-ed1c-9d6b-146064dc63ba

Business Standard, 8 January 2022, https://www.business-standard.com/article/economy-policy/first-advance-estimates-peg-fy22-gdp-growth-at-9-2-on-strong-mfg-show-122010701015_1.html

Times of India, 12 October 2021, https://timesofindia.indiatimes.com/business/india-business/india-to-grow-at-8-5-in-2022-will-retain-fastest-growing-economy-tag-imf/articleshow/86973062.cms

Narendra Modi, PMIndia.com, 17 January 2022, https://www.pmindia.gov.in/en/news_updates/pms-state-of-the-world-address-at-world-economic-forums-davos-summit/?comment=disable

Sushmi Dey, *Times of India*, 17 January 2022, https://timesofindia.indiatimes.com/india/covid-in-one-year-70-of-adults-fully-vaccinated/articleshow/88939293.cms

Ministry of Finance, Press Information Bureau, 13 December 2021, https://pib.gov.in/PressReleaseIframePage.aspx?PRID=1780999

Ashutosh Shyam, ET Mutual Funds, *Economic Times*, 12 January 2022, https://economictimes.indiatimes.com/mf/mf-news/aum-share-of-sip-linked-mutual-funds-at-a-record-high-in-december/articleshow/88831755.cms

Sanket Dhanorikar and Yogita Khatri, ET Wealth, *Economic Times*, 3 July 2017, https://economictimes.indiatimes.com/wealth/invest/why-you-should-not-stop-sip-despite-stock-market-hitting-new-highs/articleshow/59397183.cms?from=mdr

Niti Kiran, *Mint*, 5 January 2022, https://www.livemint.com/mutual-fund/mf-news/retail-investors-cling-to-mutual-funds-but-cherish-direct-investments-too-11641279604836.html

Bourree Lam, 'WSJ Journal Reports: Decade in Review', *Wall Street Journal*, 17 December 2019, https://www.wsj.com/articles/how-frugality-got-its-groove-back-11576630808

Anne Tergesen and Veronica Dagher, *Wall Street Journal*, 3 November 2018, https://www.wsj.com/articles/the-new-retirement-plan-save-almost-everything-spend-virtually-nothing-1541217688?mod=article_inline

Anand Giridharadas, *New York Times*, 18 December 2008, https://www.nytimes.com/2008/12/18/world/asia/18iht-letter.html

Saurabh Mukherjea and Anupam Gupta, *The Victory Project: Six Steps to Peak Potential*, Penguin Portfolio, 2020.

Priyanka Gawande, *Mint*, 13 January 2022, https://www.livemint.com/news/india/sebi-cracks-down-on-stock-recommendation-scam-on-telegram-11642008917450.html

Prasid Banerjee, *Mint*, 17 January 2022, https://www.livemint.com/market/cryptocurrency/crypto-scam-sites-continue-to-draw-indians-in-droves-11642359173649.html

Sucheta Dalal, Moneylife, 27 August 2020, https://www.moneylife.in/article/over-rs1000-crore-at-risk-at-anugrah-stockbrokers-and-associates/61330.html

Economic Times, 9 March 2021, https://economictimes.indiatimes.com/markets/stocks/news/sebi-imposes-rs-90-lakh-fine-on-anugrah-stock-and-broking/articleshow/81417128.cms?from=mdr

Economic Times, 11 June 2021, https://economictimes.indiatimes.com/markets/stocks/news/sensex-at-200000-likely-in-10-years-raamdeo-agrawal/articleshow/83420466.cms

Madhavankutty, *Financial Express*, 14 September 2021, https://www.financialexpress.com/economy/consistent-increase-in-household-savings-deposits-essential-for-indias-economic-growth/2329999/

Anne Tergesen and Veronica Dagher, *Wall Street Journal*, 3 November 2018, https://www.wsj.com/articles/the-new-retirement-plan-save-almost-everything-spend-virtually-nothing-1541217688

Economic Times, https://economictimes.indiatimes.com/ markets/stocks/news/sebi-imposes-rs-90-lakh-fine-on-anugrah-stock-and-broking/articleshow/81417128. cms?from=mdr

Chapter 5: A Framework for the Future

Bruce Goldman, *Scope Blog*, Stanford Medicine, 29 October 2021, https://scopeblog.stanford.edu/2021/10/29/addictive-potential-of-social-media-explained/

Subrata Panda, *Business Standard*, 12 February 2021, https://www.business-standard.com/article/economy-policy/ banks-brokers-get-most-complaints-for-mis-selling-insurance-products-121021200019_1.html